Public Relations Theory in Practice

Public Relations Theory in Practice

Strategic Applications for Professionals

Timothy Penning

BEP

BUSINESS EXPERT PRESS

Leader in applied, concise business books

Public Relations Theory in Practice:
Strategic Applications for Professionals

Cover design by Charlene Kronstedt

Interior design by S4Carlisle Publishing Services, Chennai, India

First published in 2025 by
Business Expert Press, LLC
222 East 46th Street, New York, NY 10017
www.businessexpertpress.com

ISBN-13: 978-1-63742-829-0 (paperback)
ISBN-13: 978-1-63742-830-6 (e-book)

Business Expert Press Public Relations Collection

First edition: 2025

10 9 8 7 6 5 4 3 2 1

EU SAFETY REPRESENTATIVE
Mare Nostrum Group B.V.
Mauritskade 21D
1091 GC Amsterdam
The Netherlands
gpsr@mare-nostrum.co.uk

Description

Long ago, public relations became far more than sending one-way messages and measuring success by the amount of attention gained. Today's public relations professionals need to account to management and clients for whether they have caused stakeholders to make meaningful change in their attitudes and behaviors that match organizational objectives. This requires strategy based on established *theory* that is well reasoned and tested, not just informed guesses and clever tactics.

This book is an overview of theories that are relevant to a *strategic practice* of public relations. The book begins with a simple explanation of what theories really are, how they are derived, different types of theories, and why they are practical and not mere abstractions. Chapters cover communication generally (interpersonal, small group, and organizational), mass media, persuasion, ethics, and theories specific to public relations. While grounded in academic research, each theory is concisely explained in plain language.

The emphasis is less on how the theories were made and more on how they can be *applied*. After each theory is described briefly, the book suggests how it could be applied strategically in everything from segmenting publics, to planning research, to strategic messaging, to setting campaign objectives, and counseling organizational leadership.

Contents

Testimonials

"In Public Relations Theory in Practice, *Penning does an excellent job providing an overview of the major theories applicable to public relations in easy-to-understand language. I am impressed with the breadth of theories that are addressed. The book would be a valuable resource for an undergraduate theory course or as a resource for graduate students when they are seeking theories for a specific study. It would also be a good resource for practitioners preparing for the accreditation exam (APR)."*—**Marlene S. Neill, PhD, APR, Fellow PRSA, Professor & Graduate Program Director, Senior Research Fellow, Arthur W. Page Center, Baylor University Department of Journalism, Public Relations & New Media**

"Public Relations Theory in Practice bridges the gap between academic theory and real-world application, equipping professionals with the knowledge to move beyond instinct and guesswork. Penning delves into communication, media, and persuasion and ethical theories, demonstrating how they can be strategically applied to every aspect of public relations. From understanding audiences to evaluating results, you'll learn to craft campaigns with a theoretical foundation, ensuring effectiveness and achieving organizational goals. This book is a valuable source of insight and guidance for communicators at all levels."—**Eliot Mizrachi, VP, Strategy and Content, Arthur W. Page Society**

PART I

Public Relations Theories in Practice

Years ago, I saw a comic taped to the cash register in a bookstore. The image showed two people walking with briefcases and talking. The caption said: "In theory, theory and practice are the same thing, but in practice they are not."

I laughed at the clever wordplay. But I cringed at the attitude too often expressed by professionals in any field, and, in particular, the field of public relations. As a college professor who still practices some, I often hear versions of this comic from clients and peer professionals. It usually sounds like the general sentiment "that may sound good in theory but here in the REAL world...." I have also heard a blunt dismissal such as "I'm not interested in theory."

Having worked as a public relations professional for 15 years before becoming a full-time professor for the past 25, I can personally attest to the connection between the academy and the profession. What is sad about the generally perceived disconnect between theory and practice is not just the potential insult to professors but the real opportunity cost to professionals. By dismissing theory, those who practice public relations are not availing themselves of a rich trove of strategy. It is akin to skipping the research phase of a campaign. Rather than theory being apart from practice, it is based on and intimately applies to what professionals do every day and how publics react. In every class I teach, no matter what the subject or level, I will invariably make the strong point and emphasize it in all caps on a whiteboard that "THEORY = STRATEGY." That, in a slogan, is the reason for this book.

Public Relations Theory in Practice: Strategic Applications for Professionals is written in a way intended to take the reader from a broad view to a narrow focus. Chapter 1 is an overview of the concept of theory itself to clarify and build respect for it by making it approachable and useful. The chapter covers the different types of theories, what they are based on, and how they are built. Chapter 2 surveys communication theories generally to enable better understanding of audiences. It is applicable to interactions between two people, to and within groups, and efforts to reach mass audiences. Chapter 3 is an overview of media theory, including journalism, but also other forms of media, in order to add insight to channel selection and message formation. Chapter 4 drills down on persuasion theories, to enable professionals to go beyond rudimentary attempts at gaining attention and awareness to effect positive change in attitude and behavior. Given the potential for abuse of persuasion, Chapter 5 is devoted to ethical theories, from classical ethics philosophically to specific public relations ethics theories and decision-making models. Finally, with public relations drawing from other disciplines for much of its theory, Chapter 6 is focused on theory specific to public relations in a way that elevates public relations from mere tactical output to a management-level profession.

The book is written to be useful to current and aspiring public relations professionals. While entire books have been written about single theories, this book maintains the goals of brevity and practicality. It gives the basic premise of each theory and its strategic and practical application in a public relations context. It can be useful to read the whole book as a review of or introduction to theory, or it can serve as a desk reference to consult a specific section when seeking to make wise and strategic decisions, whether forming research questions, writing objectives, planning strategies and messages, selecting appropriate tactics, or evaluating results.

I would hope that after reading the book, professionals will, unlike the characters in the comic, conclude that theory and practice are the same thing and also that the practice of public relations is more strategic, effective, and enjoyable when theory is applied.

CHAPTER 1

Theories—How They Are Made and Why They Are Useful in Daily Practice

Noted psychologist Kurt Lewin is credited with asserting several times and in several ways the principle that "there is nothing so practical as a good theory" (Lewin 1943). If that is true, then there should not be the disconnect between theory and practice that has been observed. Academics assert that there should be, in keeping with public relations, a "mutually beneficial relationship" among scholars and professionals, that scholarship should be valued and adopted by practitioners whose experiences would further validate research (Hayes et al. 2023), and for this reason "theory and practice are inextricably intertwined" (Travis and Lordan 2021, 1). Theory is more than an abstraction, and actually unavoidable. "Theory is correlated with life, the world, people and society. It is constructed in order to explain them systematically and coherently. There is an obligatory and indispensable relationship between theory and practice" (Akim 2018, 217).

Other academics point out that professionals use theory, "whether they realize it or not" (Brunner 2019, 1). For example, when professionals comment on how they do something at work repeatedly because it is consistently successful, they are articulating a theory, albeit a basic one (Dainton and Zelley 2023). Because of this, practitioners can and should take ownership of the knowledge of the field and not let it be distinctive to academics (Bowman and Hendy 2019). In fact, practitioners and academics both build theory—academics through research that includes observation of large numbers of professionals and practitioners by sharing and codifying their experience (Brunner 2019).

However, the disconnect continues. This is attributed in part to the somewhat abstract topics that academics select to study and by the "ineffective translation of academic research into publications, frameworks and tools that practitioners can use" (Claeys and Opgenhoffen 2016, 233). Another problem is that practitioners cannot access the academic journals where most academic research is shared. Meanwhile, a review of trade publications in public relations showed that fewer than 1 percent cite academic research, much less theory (Marla and Callison 2012). Ironically, there is limited research on public relations practitioners' views of theory, although one recent study found that they view research as casual and informal versus scientific. They see most relevant research being that done by peer professionals and little need for an underlying basis of theoretical knowledge. Practitioners know of theory, generally, but value it in principle and not in application (Hayes et al. 2023). For example, in a crisis communications context, professionals sought tailor-made guidelines, as opposed to typologies from theory. Some used gut feelings, while others combined theory with their own experience to respond to a crisis (Claeys and Opgenhoffen 2016).

The disconnect is not for lack of trying. The study guide for the *Accreditation in Public Relations* (APR) exam has a section on communication theories, models, and the history of the profession (Public Relations Society of America 2021). Fully 10 percent of the exam for the Certificate in Principles of Public Relations is on theory (Public Relations Society of America 2024). The Commission on Education in Public Relations (CEPR), made up of professors and professionals who make recommendations for university public relations curricula, had a chapter on theory in its 2017 report and, in a survey in its 2023 report, noted that close to an equal number of educators and professionals said a knowledge of public relations theory is desired for college graduates. The six-course standard recommended by the CEPR includes research, writing, campaigns, case studies, internships, and ethics, but does not include a course exclusively on theory, although knowledge of theory ranked somewhere in the middle of all areas of knowledge desired by academics as well as professionals (Commission on Education in Public Relations 2023).

Not all public relations practitioners have a degree in public relations. If they did, they were introduced only to a few theories, they were not taught to apply them, or they simply did not remember them. Regardless of a professional's academic background, the key to applying theory to practice is to have an accurate understanding of what a theory is, how it is made, the different types of theories, what constitutes a "good" theory, and how exactly they can be applied.

What Is a Theory? What Is a Good Theory?

"Theory" is one of those words that people think they understand intuitively until they really think about it. Even academics will say it is difficult to find a preferred explanation of communication theory (van Ruler 2018). Fundamentally, theories provide a perspective to see the world and are an agreed upon aspect of reality, not just abstract concepts (Dainton and Zelley 2023). Again, there is a disconnect between professionals and scholars in valuing theory because of a divergent understanding of what theory is. Broadly speaking, *a theory is any attempt to represent or explain a phenomenon*, but "the word theory can be used to describe the educated guesswork of laypersons … [but] a theory is the scholar's construction of what an experience is like based on [a] system of observation" (Littlejohn 1989, 2). A professional may have years of experience, which is valid, but it is only one person's experience and hard to generalize. A scholarly approach to theory can be more confidently applied broadly because it is based on observations of many individuals in real contexts (Hazelton and Botan 1999).

When it comes to communication, specifically, there is an entire body of theories that comprise an understanding of the complex communication process and, in particular, how the process of creating meaning works (van Ruler 2018). Putting it another way, a communication theory is a systematic summary of the communication process (Dainton and Zelley 2023). A key element of theories with regard to explaining a process is the explanation of *causal relationships* (Travis and Lordan 2021). In other words, theories explain and predict real phenomena by determining what causes them. Sometimes, the word "model" is used. This can be a synonym for theory but is best understood as a visual representation of what a theory says. It can also be developed as a precursor to a theory or be the output application of a theory (Dainton and Zelley 2023).

It is important to acknowledge that not all theories are the same in their quality and usefulness. There are numerous academic typologies of what makes for a good theory (Dainton and Zelly 2023; Littlejohn 1989; Travis and Lordan 2021). They commonly refer to: accuracy in terms of reflecting the phenomenon they address and that research and testing supports that the theory works; simplicity and brevity in terms of logic and number of concepts; and practicality in terms of real-world application, making the complex understandable, able to be generalized, and widely applied. Good theories are also *dynamic* in that they are open to challenges and refinement over time. Public relations theories (and those applied to public relations from other fields) range in terms of how "good" they are according to these criteria. Many public relations theories are said to be "middle range" (as opposed to general) because they make explanations and applications to specific settings or contexts of practice. But there are also general theories, which result from propositions that are tested and which explain broader phenomena (Brunner 2019).

Different Types of Theories

Theory can be misunderstood and therefore undervalued because of confusion caused by the fact that there are different types of theories. Each type of theory has a different method of development and a different type of value. As noted previously, professionals may develop theory when they assemble and apply practical ideas, a form of theory known as "operational" or "everyday" theory (McQuail and Deuze 2020).

Another form of theory that is the common perception of laypersons is derived from reason and philosophy. This is known as *cultural or humanistic theory*, and it tends to be subjective, creative, offering alternative explanations but resistant to quantitative testing (McQuail and Deuze 2020; Littlejohn 1989). *Critical theory* is related to cultural theory and has the element of values brought to bear on interpretation and assertions. With regard to communication and public relations, critical theory seeks to expose problems and faults in media and communication practice and relate them to social issues (Windahl et al. 2007).

Normative theory is so called because it seeks to create norms of behavior in society or in a particular profession. Rather than describing phenomena, normative theory examines and offers prescriptions for how people ought to act. Examples of this would be ethical theory, typologies for crisis communication, or models for public relations practice that is deemed "excellent" and a proposed standard of practice.

Scientific or social scientific theories are those that follow a standardized process of objective observation and interpretation. While previous forms of theories are based on reason and subjective assertion, scientific theories are based on evidence and objective explanation and prediction. Note that predictions are often with regard to patterns and likelihood, not absolute and universal cause and effect. This is the case in physical science as well as social science. Due to individual variance, each person may respond differently to a medication or a message. This variance is said to be within subjects—one individual responds differently on separate occasions—or between subjects—different individuals respond differently. But when data shows a significant number respond in the same way to a causal variable or combination of them, and not by random chance, a scientific theory demonstrates its value.

Theories in communication can also be classified according to the context about which they focus. These include structural and functional, cognitive and behavioral, interactional and conversational, and interpretive and critical (Littlejohn 1989). Structural and functional theories look at the impact of society as a structure, with interrelated parts, on communication. Cognitive and behavioral theory looks at how communication affects and is a result of how people think and act. Interactional and conversational theory puts the focus on the process of communication itself. Interpretive and critical theory looks at the larger meaning of communication in terms of fairness and equity, or how communication is enabling or causes harm to individuals and society.

How Theories Are Made

There is a common expression that is a reflection of a misunderstanding of how theories are made. "You can't prove theory" is a statement uttered to dismiss the relevance of theory. This is a true statement technically, but it is misapplied to theories derived using the scientific method. A few of the foregoing theories cannot be proven because they are based on reason and observation of single episodes or small samples, or the purpose of the theory is to assert the way things should be rather than to describe how they are. Scientific theories also are not "proven" per se because the process is to attempt to disprove them.

Scientific theory is a form of deductive theory in which hypotheses—statements of association or prediction—are developed based on observation of numerous examples. Researchers determine the best method (experiment, survey, etc.) to test the hypothesis. They then conduct that research test and interpret the results. In scientific research, sample size and effect size are important considerations. A larger sample means the results are more likely to be reliable and consistently the same when tried repeatedly with different groups and are therefore generalizable. Effect size reflects how significant a relationship is between variables of cause and effect. A large effect size is more practical because predictions can be made with confidence.

Hypothesis statements include independent variables (causes) and dependent variables (effects). Statements can also be called propositions, axioms, postulates, or theorems. Falsification, or attempting to disprove hypotheses (also called an attempt to prove the "null" or opposite hypothesis) has been part of the scientific method since the mid-1900s (Popper 1959). If a researcher cannot prove the null hypothesis, then the hypothesis must be true. Usually this is determined by a statistic called a "confidence interval," which is a reflection of how likely some observed cause–effect relationship did not happen by chance. Statistically, a result is valid at a confidence interval of 99 percent or 95 percent, or, put another way, only a 1 percent or 5 percent chance that the result was due to random error. In other words, theories are not proven—they are validated when their hypotheses cannot be disproven. Advanced statistics are used to determine if results are significant and worthy of theoretical propositions. Insignificant results require new propositions, perhaps consideration of other variables, and further testing. A statistically significant result means there is a solid foundation on which to build theory and that the results are valid and reliable and therefore applicable to theory building and practical application.

When considering a theory and its application, it is always useful to be mindful of the type of theory it is and how it was derived. A professional should consider all theories to be interesting but also determine if they are generalizable to their own context and therefore relevant for application. All theories have value, but the value of a theory is different based on how it was derived, whether it is midlevel (based on a specific context) or general (able to apply broadly). That said, some midlevel theories have yet to be tested in other specific contexts and may in time prove value as a general theory. Given the different types of theory, their practical application may vary accordingly. But there are certainly practical benefits of theory, particularly given the recent demand for public relations professionals to demonstrate behavioral outcomes that contribute to overall organizational success in ways distinct from other functions.

The Practical Benefits of Theory

This chapter started with the assertion from psychologist Kurt Lewin that nothing is more practical than a good theory. The question is why. The answers are also practical.

Consider the types and bases of theory. If a professional knows the result of volumes of research in real contexts, if they know that a predictive statement has been scientifically tested and shown to be statistically significant, reliable, and generalizable, why would they not seek to capitalize on it? Many public relations managers aspire to having a "seat at the table" or to be part of management decision making, not just those charged with communicating the decisions made by others. A knowledge of theory and how to apply it is the path to that management-level involvement. It does not necessarily mean explaining the details of theory to a CEO, but confidently articulating the concepts and predicting results can be the basis of wise counsel. As one scholar asserted, "If public relations practitioners want to participate in decision making, they need training that provides both theoretical and practical knowledge and skill" (Akim 2018, 217). Theory is how a public relations professional's efforts become strategic because they are focused on the results among publics more than creativity of tactics. A knowledge of theory helps professionals explain public relations in management terms to organizational leaders: "only communication that has the intention to advance an organization's mission can be defined as strategic" (van Ruler 2018, 372).

Theory is not something to be taken into consideration only on occasion. It should be rooted and embedded in everything in the public relations process, from understanding publics, to creating messaging, developing strategy, implementing tactics, and evaluating results. Theory helps professionals focus attention, clarify concepts, predict outcomes, and generate personal and social change (Dainton and Zelley 2023). Theory should be important to practitioners and educators alike because "without theory, we base our decisions on instinct" (Brunner 2019, 3). It should not be difficult to choose between approaching a public relations task with a dart and blindfold or a proven record of hitting the bull's-eye.

Overview of Rest of the Book

The practical benefits of theory become more obvious with specific knowledge of individual theories and categories of theories. The remaining chapters of the book, in order to remain brief and practical, will not dive into the details of how each theory mentioned was developed. Instead, the focus will be on the essence of what the theory describes or predicts and how it associates concepts. The reader can trust that the theories have been "proven" in terms of the method by which they were developed, how they have withstood repeated testing in real-world scenarios, or how often they have been cited by academics as they are applied to multiple contexts. Along with the explanation of each of the theories, there is guidance for practical application.

The theories in the remaining chapters are logically ordered according to practical tasks a public relations professional would have to address in a typical day. In other words, each category of theories relates to a category of public relations practice. The categories are introduced in an order related to concentric circles from fundamental to applied, from broadly about communications to focused on the field of public relations.

Part II offers an overview of general communication theories, from interpersonal to group to organizational to intercultural. These theories all relate to the public relations concern with understanding audiences, how they think and behave and communicate and respond to communication in different contexts. These theories are relevant to professionals who want

Communication

Media

Persuasion

Ethics

Public
Relations

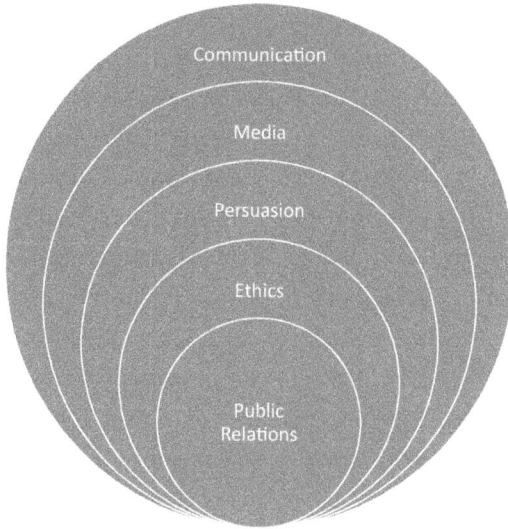

to think more specifically and strategically about the accepted wisdom of the importance of knowing one's audience before communicating.

Part III narrows the focus from communication to media theories. These theories are very useful to consider by public relations professionals when they desire to choose appropriate communication channels and use them effectively. Media is defined broadly in terms of news media, in particular, but also any form or method that mediates messages between individuals, groups, and organizations. The media theories range from one-way news media theories, to theories about the effects of media, to computer-mediated and social media and dialogic communication theories. Such theories will help professionals go beyond a rudimentary "get the word out" tactical output performance to a more measured and strategic use of media of all types with the objective of reaching relevant audiences in ways that earn their attention.

Part IV narrows the scope of theories even more to focus on persuasion. While mass and interpersonal media can be used to meet a low-level goal of raising awareness, persuasion is a more difficult objective to achieve. But there is a body of theories that explain and aid professionals in attempts to get attention in a society saturated with information and also to affect attitude, opinion, motivation, and action by the recipients of messages. Knowledge and application of this category of theory is directly related to message strategy and outcome objectives.

Because persuasion can be criticized for being manipulative, Chapter 5 offers a necessary look at a good companion to persuasion theory: ethical theory. Persuasion in itself is not unethical, but how it is done may be. Given the nature of ethics, these theories tend to be normative in nature. The chapter starts with an overview of some classical theories of ethics from the ancient to modern philosophers, continues with modern ethical theory related specifically to the practice of public relations, and concludes with some practical models for ethical decision making. While ethics can seem esoteric, these theories have abundant practical value for practitioners who seek to be professional in their practice, not to mention to avoid a crisis of public opinion or legal consequences. A knowledge and application of ethics is fundamental to risk management and crisis communication strategy in this regard.

While public relations scholars and professionals can learn and apply theories from many other fields of study and practice, the book concludes with a very narrow focus in Chapter 6 on theories particular to public relations. These categories of theories are organized into models for public relations practice, theories about professional roles in public relations, and theories of relationship and engagement. Professionals will have benefited from previous chapters and concepts on communication, sociology, and psychology. But the concluding chapter will positively affect how they conceive of what public relations really is and how it can best be practiced. Knowledge of these public relations theories should generate both pride in the profession and confidence in practicing it.

Again, the purpose of this book is not only to help public relations professionals to understand theory but also to enable them to apply theory specifically as strategies for public relations practice. With that in mind, each part will end with a strategic summary, including specific statements about how a professional should think about and perform their job.

Strategic Summary of Part I—Theory

Part I is a general overview of theories and some ways they are not just abstractions but useful in the daily practice of public relations. Here are some strategic insights about theory and practice, in general:

- Theories are based on the rigorous and scientific observations and testing of actual human interactions, including public relations practice. Theory is not separate from a perceived "real world" but has a more valid explanation of it than individual experience.
- The most fundamental practical benefit of theory is its ability to predict when and why people pay attention to messages and how they respond (i.e., behave).
- Public relations professionals may actually articulate theory without realizing it when they explain they are doing something because they are predicting a desired result.
- Professionals and academics alike have expressed the value of understanding theory to enhance the quality of practice.
- All theory has value, but that value may vary based on the type of theory and how it was derived.
- Midlevel theories are about specific contexts, whereas general theories are more broadly applicable.
- The statement "theories cannot be proven" is misleading. Theory development by scientific method involves trying to disprove a hypothesis, and if that fails, the cause–effect relationship in the hypothesis is said to be valid and not caused by random chance.
- Knowledge of theory can also help a public relations professional better understand the essence of public relations and explain it in management terms to clients and organizational leaders.

PART II

Communication Theories—Understanding Audiences

Public relations is a communication discipline, so a foundational understanding of communication theories is important for professionals who practice public relations. Public relations is more specific than communications in that it involves particular forms of communication. But it is also broader than communication because public relations has larger end goals or objectives relative to the organizations public relations professionals serve. In other words, communication is a means to an end, but public relations' objectives are the end.

For communication, including public relations, to be successful, it is a fundamental principle that communicators should know their audience. But strategically that should go beyond just knowing who and where they are. Theory helps professionals know more about audience attitudes and the reason for them, what gets their attention and moves them to respond, how to appeal to values appropriately, how to interpret meaning, and more. Therefore, a chapter of theory related to understanding audiences must begin with some theoretical discussion of the basic concept of audiences.

CHAPTER 2

Interpersonal Theories

Public relations scholars make distinctions between audiences, publics, and stakeholders. Understanding these distinctions is important theoretically and strategically. Traditionally, audiences are passive recipients of messages, whereas the term "publics" implies that there is a relationship involved. The idea of a public or collective entity with legitimacy to act on politics, economy, and culture is rooted in the Protestant Reformation and the Enlightenment in seventeenth century England and is reflected in modern democratic governments (Pieczka 2019). Philosophical views distinguish between *the* public—an ideal abstract concept—and *a* public—which is concrete, embodied, and has multiple variations. In the early 1900s, philosophers John Dewey and Jurgen Habermas considered publics to be reason-based, reflective, and collaborative. Journalist Walter Lippman and early public relations pioneer Edward Bernays doubted the possibility of a cohesive public and asserted that experts were needed to manage public affairs (Pieczka 2019). Today, it is common for strategic public relations professionals to say there is no "general" public, and good practice is generally understood to involve segmenting publics by demographics, needs, and other factors.

Meanwhile, the term stakeholder was defined as "any group or individual who can affect or is affected by the achievement of the organization's objectives" (Freeman 1984, 46). Stakeholders are distinct and not interchangeable with publics. Stakeholder theory will be discussed in Part 5 on ethics, but for now it is important to understand the term relative to other concepts about the recipients of public relations messages or those with whom organizations build relationships.

Scholars have conceived of stakeholders as having a relationship to the *organization*, while publics have a relationship to an *issue* (Rawlins 2006). Others argue that organizations choose stakeholders, but publics arise on their own and choose the organization for attention

(Grunig and Repper 1992). The perspective that publics are autonomous is even more valid in the era of social media, in which audiences have been said to connect to a message and react to it, while stakeholders connect to an organization and seek to sustain it, and publics connect to issues and seek to affect change (Wakefield and Knighton 2019).

Given the changing landscape of communication, technology, and culture, scholars have recently called for an even closer examination of how public relations professionals view and interact with people for the improvement of both theory and practice: "A more nuanced understanding of the organization and its stakeholders is necessary in order to align public relations theory with the intricate realities of practice" (Page and Capizzo 2024, 1). In other words, organizing stakeholders on simplistic internal/external frameworks is not enough. An alternative perspective would take a legal view to see organizations as complex legal entities and stakeholders having multiple identities and engaging in both formal and informal "contracts" in interacting with organizations. Given this perspective, it would be acceptable if professionals did not treat all stakeholders equally.

Understanding audiences theoretically begins with understanding the concepts of audience, public, and stakeholder. Doing so will change not just with whom a public relations professional interacts but how and why. The theories that follow in this chapter will further facilitate that. The theories are organized into categories according to scope of interaction, from interpersonal, to small group, to organizational, to intercultural, which reflect the different communication situations in which a professional will work in a given day. Note that some theories, while assigned to a certain context, could be applied in multiple communication contexts from interpersonal to intercultural.

Public relations professionals will often find themselves communicating with one other person, or a few other individuals. This could be in a situation of hiring an employee, negotiating with an activist, lobbying a government official, pitching to a journalist, speech training an executive, or meeting with a potential donor. Theorists call such one-on-one interactions *dyadic* communication. The theories that follow provide insight on what is really going on in such instances beyond a mere exchange of words.

Shannon-Weaver Model

One of the oldest communications theories came from a mathematician and an electrical engineer who wrote an article titled *A Mathematical Model of Communications* for a Bell System publication (Shannon and Weaver 1949). Typical of engineers, their model breaks down communication interactions into a sequence of steps in a process. There is a sender who encodes a message into signals and transmits it through a channel where a receiver decodes the signals to understand the message. The concept of "noise" is anything that distorts or masks the signal.

While it seems simplistic, today it is useful to be reminded of these concepts and be strategic when encoding signals and selecting channels to increase the chances that they will be received and properly decoded. It is naïve to assume that all people will understand a message exactly how a professional wants it to be understood. "Encoding" with clarity, relevance, and respect will more likely lead to proper "decoding." Public relations professionals must also be mindful of potential noise, which could include competing or contradictory messages or just other demands on a recipient's attention in certain times, contexts, and channels. The model can be interpreted as not merely singular, transactional interactions but an ongoing process of sender and receiver (public relations professional and audiences) negotiating noise to achieve an engagement. Subsequent theories will address degrees of attention and response.

Symbolic Interactionism

The essence of *symbolic interactionism* as a theory is that "an individual's perception of reality and behavior is shaped by social exchanges and communication, particularly language and subjective meaning assigned to symbols" (Travis and Lordan 2021, 44). In other words, humans act toward physical or abstract objects that have meanings assigned to them on the basis of interaction with others, and these meanings can change based on interactions with other members of society. A professional can learn and use the fact that meaning is in more than words alone.

Symbolic interactionism can also be applied to the organizational level as companies, nonprofits, and government entities (e.g., congresses, agencies, departments) interact with individuals. Each individual, and the collective efforts of other people, lead to the structures and processes of organizations. A blunt way of saying it is that "social reality is what people think it is" (Prior-Miller 1989, 70). Or public relations professionals have less control over communication processes than they may sometimes assume.

However, a professional could gain some strategy and confidence in communication with a more complete description of symbolic interactionism, which includes seven basic concepts:

1. Humans behave and interact through symbols and meanings;
2. Individuals are humanized through interactions with others;
3. Society is a process of people in interaction;
4. Humans actively shape their own behavior;
5. Conscious thought involves interacting with one's self;
6. People construct their behavior in the course of an interaction; and
7. Understanding conduct requires the study of a person's current behavior (Manis and Melzer 1978).

Given this theory and its seven concepts, public relations professionals should consider that there is more to any interpersonal interaction than a back and forth of words. Ahead of and during any such interaction, professionals can strategically consider what symbols they are sending, consciously or otherwise, that provide the meaning to the public of interest. These symbols can be words, gestures, other nonverbal communicators, the context or setting of the interaction, and more. The meaning may be and often is different than the words because whomever was speaking did not think of the subtle symbols that may have drowned out the actual words. In fact, one scholar cautions against considering the word or symbol actually being that which it describes, in the same way that an area on a map is not actually the territory it represents (Kozybski 1933). It is wise to consider the organization as one part of the environment and that communication is continuous and not happening only when the organization is involved. Also, the public is in control of interpreting meaning, so some research on existing public knowledge and attitude is always useful to strategically and appropriately frame messages.

Exchange Theory

Exchange theory, also called *social exchange theory*, "explains and predicts an individual's decision to maintain or deescalate a particular relationship" (Thibaut and Kelley 1959, 56). The theory makes the assumption that humans are self-interested and weigh personal relationships in terms of costs and benefits. This analysis considers the basic outcome value, or basic rewards and costs of the relationship. In addition, an individual would consider a comparison level of expected rewards in a given relationship, as well as a comparison level of alternative relationships, to determine whether to maintain the relationship. Sustaining or ending a relationship is related to communication directly—communication will occur only in a *sustained* relationship.

Professionals should refrain from seeing each interaction as an opportunity for themselves to get a message out and instead be mindful of how those to whom they communicate are evaluating the relationship and interaction. For example, before communicating, professionals should ask themselves how the public in question might expect to benefit from interacting and what might make a relationship costly to the public. Increasing the frequency and urgency of messages misses the mark. Having interactions and framing messages in a way that rewards audiences will maintain the relationship and ensure ongoing, positive communication. Several theories in later chapters will further illuminate the concept of relationships as a strategic framework and the essence of the public relations profession.

Uncertainty Reduction Theory

Uncertainty reduction theory applies mostly to two individuals in their initial interaction. The uncertainty in the theory means an inability to predict or explain their own or the other's behavior or thoughts. Humans do not like uncertainty or unknowns and use verbal and nonverbal communication, as well as intimate levels of content, to reduce that uncertainty. There are three reasons a person might be motivated to reduce uncertainty or get to know the other. These include an expectation of future encounters, anticipation of a reward from the relationship, or experiencing unexpected behavior from the other person (Travis and Lordan 2021).

Individuals adopt several strategies to reduce uncertainty. A passive strategy would be to observe the other, an active strategy would be to seek information about the other from a third party, and an interactive strategy would be to ask for information directly from the other person in the interaction (Berger and Calabrese 1975). It is not unlike a personal dating scenario in which someone is contemplating asking another on a date but does some "research" to reduce uncertainty first by observing a person, asking a friend about them, and, finally, having a direct conversation with the other person and asking some questions.

The theory includes eight axioms that can be considered when engaging in interpersonal communications:

1. As nonverbal communication increases, uncertainty decreases;
2. Welcoming nonverbal expressions decreases uncertainty;
3. Greater uncertainty leads to more information seeking;
4. High uncertainty leads to low intimacy level in the interaction;
5. More uncertainty leads to reciprocal communication strategies (a give and take in the interaction);
6. More perceived similarities between the two individuals leads to less feeling of uncertainty;
7. As uncertainty decreases, "liking" of the other person increases; and
8. Shared communication networks or ties reduce uncertainty (Dainton and Zelley 2023, 38).

Professionals who encounter someone who seems unresponsive or reticent in an interpersonal interaction could address the situation strategically by applying concepts listed in the axioms to reduce potential uncertainty. For example, a professional could be intentional about the use of nonverbal cues, foreground similarities and common ground, and use shared communication networks (e.g., social media, in-person, e-mail exchanges). A general premise for practice also emerges from this theory—taking the time to build a relationship before communicating can yield better results in terms of people receiving and responding to messages. Addressing the uncertainty of the other will reduce barriers to communication and understanding.

Relational Framing Theory

Relational framing theory, in essence, states that people interpret messages by focusing on one of two frames for the nature of the relationship—dominance/submissiveness or affiliation/disaffiliation (Dillard and Salomon 2005). The dominance/submissiveness frame has to do with how one person attempts to control the behavior of another, either directly or by status. The affiliation/disaffiliation is about how much appreciation or esteem one holds for the other. Both frames are not either/or but exist on a range. Frames in this theory are "mental structures consisting of organized knowledge about social relationships" (Solomon et al. 2002, 137). If the two frames seem at odds, the one more relevant to the perceived purpose of the interaction is the one attended to in a given episode or interaction. The dominance/submissiveness frame is more relevant in situations where one is seeking compliance. If building a relationship or trust is the goal, then the affiliation/disaffiliation frame is more relevant.

The theory applies mostly to individuals with some anxiety about the relationship. In established and positive relationships, the focus is more on content than relational frames. Again, it can be seen how perceptions about the nature of a relationship signal more than actual words in a communication interaction and affect the interpretation of messages. Professionals, especially in initial interactions or new relationships, can apply this theory by considering the goal of the communication and how the recipient will frame the relationship on these two scales and which scale is relevant in a given interaction. Use of nonverbal cues and carefully chosen words to enhance affiliation and reduce unintended perceptions of dominance will help communication to be received, understood, and responded to in a manner consistent with goals for the interaction.

Power Dependence Theory

As the name implies, *power dependence theory* views the power balance in interpersonal relationships as a major factor in communication. The theory analyzes the interplay between dependency on the relationship, the level of power each person has in the relationship, and the use of power. Note that later in this book, the concepts of symmetrical communication and control mutuality will be addressed as concepts important for ethical and strategic public relations practice. For now, the basics of this theory state that the more dependent a person is on a social relationship, the less power that person has. At the same time, the theory proposes that the use of power in the relationship increases with an imbalance of dependencies— i.e., one person depends on the relationship more than the other (Emerson 1962).

The theory almost has an economic flavor in its propositions. The more a person values resources (money, information, connections) controlled by another, the more dependent they are. The more those resources are available outside the relationship from another source, the less dependent a person is. Less dependent people are said to have a power advantage, while more dependent people are considered power imbalanced. The greater the asymmetry in the communication between two people, the more power will be exerted in that interaction (Molm 1985).

Four power balancing mechanisms have been suggested (Emerson 1962), although it is usually the person with lower power who will desire to use them. The lower-powered person can reduce the value they place on the resources controlled by the other or seek alternative sources for those resources. The high-power individual, should they decide altruistically or strategically to reduce the power imbalance, could place higher value on resources controlled by the other. Or the high-power individual could be denied alternative sources of resources to equalize power and add symmetry to the relationship.

The theory is useful to professionals to plan interpersonal interactions by considering real or perceived power imbalances that may be influencing how and how much people contribute to communication. They could also verbalize some of the strategies to equalize the power imbalance in a relationship in order to have a more fluid, positive, and productive interaction.

CHAPTER 3

Small Group Theories

Public relations professionals often have to communicate to and within groups. It could be a team at an agency or an in-house public relations department. It could be other groups internal to the organization, such as investors or employees, or it could be external groups ranging from consumer categories to local communities to activist groups. Group communication, theoretically, is an extension of interpersonal communication, because many of the group interactions and processes involve dyadic pairs communicating interpersonally within a group context.

There are a variety of categories of theory related to small group communication. Looking broadly, each general theoretical perspective of small groups can be considered by professionals when planning how to approach communicating to or within a group.

The *functional perspective* is a normative view that assumes groups are goal oriented and predicts and describes group performance based on inputs and processes within groups. Inputs include the nature of the task the group is assigned, composition of the group in terms of member characteristics, internal structure of the group, and the group's environment in the organization and industry. These affect outputs such as productivity, efficiency, leadership of the group, leadership effectiveness, and satisfaction with group outcomes. Professionals can factor these inputs when planning communication to and within groups.

The *psychodynamic perspective* of group theory works backward to emphasize process and outcomes and considers inputs to groups a secondary concern. This perspective examines the relationship between emotional and nonconscious processes and the rational and conscious processes of interactions in groups. Professionals can strategically consider how communication is affected by group processes such as meeting management, leadership style, brainstorming, soliciting input, and more.

The *social identity perspective* looks at groups in terms of how individuals identify with groups to which they belong with a focus on relations between different groups. Professionals should be mindful of each member's sense of belonging to a group.

The *conflict–power–status perspective* assumes inequality among group members and is therefore concerned with group processes that affect influence, conflict management and negotiation, and consensus building. A wise approach in this case is to work on group culture prior to other messaging.

The *social network perspective* considers groups to be part of a larger network and studies patterns of relationships among group members. Strategic consideration and engagement with subgroups can be effective for communication as a result of this perspective.

Finally, the *temporal perspective* emphasizes process and looks at how groups change over time. Communicators should be mindful of group history when planning communication and seek to leverage it and not harm group response by ignoring it (Poole and Hollingshead 2005).

The small group theories chosen in this section include a variety of these perspectives and are among the most commonly cited in academic literature and most applicable to public relations practice.

Groupthink

The essence of *groupthink theory* is that group members' strivings for unanimity override their motivation to realistically appraise alternative courses of action" (Janis 1982, 9). Another way of saying it is "at its core, the notion of groupthink represents a failure of the group to demonstrate critical thinking" (Dainton and Zelley 2023, 150). Practically, what this means is that no individual speaks up or pushes back because they perceive a group consensus or that they are the only one thinking differently, when, in fact, others may also have different views than what is expressed by the group. An astute group leader or member can see the conditions that are right for groupthink: a solidarity, homogeneity, and cohesion of members; a group that is insulated from outside input or with a biased leader; no procedural norms; or a stressful situation. Symptoms of a group in danger of groupthink include an inflated view of the group's abilities, a closed-mindedness and polarized thinking, and pressure to conform to uniformity (Dainton and Zelley 2023).

Irving Janis, the originator of groupthink theory, spells out six negative outcomes and nine steps to prevent groupthink. The negative outcomes include limiting discussion to only a few options; failure to review the group's initial position for flaws; the group fails to examine alternatives not in favor by the majority in the group; no expert opinion from outside the group is sought; the group is selective in gathering and attending to relevant information; the group is overconfident and does not consider contingencies or consequences of its chosen action or statement (Janis 1982).

The nine steps or group communication processes to strategically prevent groupthink proposed by Janis are as follows:

1. The leader gives priority to individual members' expression of doubt or criticism;
2. The leaders should not state expectations for specific decisions when assigning a task to the group;
3. Different groups can be assigned to deliberate separately;
4. A group can be divided into subgroups and then reconvene to share and consider alternative solutions;
5. Each member can discuss group deliberations with trusted outsiders;
6. Bring in outside experts on a staggered basis;
7. Assign one member at every meeting the role of devil's advocate;
8. Survey warning signals from rivals and conduct alternative scenarios; and
9. Before finalizing a decision, give every member a final chance to express doubts or rethink the issue (Janis 1982).

Janis' steps are practically helpful as a collection of process ideas for public relations professionals in many group contexts. An ordered problem-solving process for group decision making was offered years ago by John Dewey:

1. Express a difficulty;
2. Define the problem;
3. Analyze the problem;

4. Suggest a number of solutions;

5. Compare and test alternatives against objectives; and

6. Implement one solution chosen out of this process (Dewey 1910).

Professionals should want confidence that groups make the best decision. This could be a team at an agency or in-house public relations department, or it could be any external group with whom a professional works to represent an organization. Strategically detecting, preventing, and correcting groupthink can lead to more successful group outcomes.

Functional Theory of Group Decision Making

While groupthink offers steps to avoid this negative group phenomenon, the *functional theory of group decision making* offers another similar stepwise approach that is general in nature and focused on positive outcomes. The theory is focused on what groups actually do, as opposed to what each member thinks. It proposes that "effective group decision making is contingent on interactions contributing to the satisfaction of critical task requirements" (Hollingshead et al. 2005, 26). While the success of group decision making can vary due to the complexity of the issue at hand, the nature of the task, and group composition, a five-step process in this theory can help to predict an increased likelihood of positive outcome of group decision making:

1. Develop thorough, accurate understanding of the problem (its nature, seriousness, cause, and other aspects);

2. Achieve an understanding of what would make a decision acceptable to those evaluating the decision, including client, management, or publics of interest;

3. Develop a range of realistic, acceptable solutions;

4. Assess and describe the merits and positive consequences of each alternative choice developed; and

5. Assess negative consequences of each choice (Hollingshead et al. 2005).

Following this process and with resulting information, groups can make a reasoned decision with a greater likelihood of success. One study testing this theory by a meta-analysis of multiple related studies found that three of the five steps were the most important factors, with assessment of negative consequences being the most important. Problem analysis and criteria development were the other most important. Time spent brainstorming and generating alternative solutions was least important but still helpful (Orlitzky and Hirokawa 2001).

The application of this theory is clear for professionals who can be intentional about following steps when faced with a decision to make. A public relations professional could be leading the group or simply one member of it. Either way, this theory could be a basis for suggestions to improve group process and communication. Each situation will be different, as noted previously, but an ordered format for a group's work can be more strategic than calling a meeting and uttering a general call for ideas without a strategic procedure.

Social Identity Theory

Social identity theory deals with how an individual perceives of themselves relative to others, including the groups to which they belong. There are three aspects of the self: individual personal traits that differentiate one from others; relational identity is the way one assimilates to others via relationships; and collective identity is about how group members differentiate "us" from "them" or their group from others (Abrams et al. 2005). Sometimes, the most meaningful identity for a person has to do with the groups to which one belongs, and stereotypes in this sense are shared and may serve a positive social function as individual identities become self-categorizations (Tajfel 1981). Social identity is directly related to how people communicate in group contexts: "when social identity is salient, group members strive for positive distinctiveness for their group. By ensuring that their ingroup is positively distinctive from outgroups, the ingroup, and hence the self, is imbued with positive value" (Abrams et al. 2005, 108).

Another way of viewing this is that social identification describes how much a person considers relationship with another person or group to be part of their own identity. In fact, a person's self-concept is a combination of their personal identity and social identity. Both are complex.

A personal identity includes characteristics, values, attitudes, beliefs, and traits. A social identity can include race, employer, faith, geographic residence, and a myriad of other groups to which someone belongs (Ashforth and Mael 1989). A specific form of social identification is *organizational identification*—this could be the overall organization or a specific subgroup within an organization.

There are many reasons a professional working with groups should be mindful of the concept of social identity. Communicating in ways that acknowledge or actively foster social identity with groups can be more successful in terms of attention and response. Each public can be seen and addressed in terms of how their interaction with an organization or related group affects their social identity. Social identity theory can be applied to socialization or onboarding new employees, building and maintaining organizational culture, developing and working with brand ambassadors, incorporating identity message strategies in internal communications or to select other external publics, and working to ensure that social identity with subgroups is consistent with that of the organization. For example, employees of large groups may have a strong and positive identification with their work team or department even as they have a minor or even negative identification with the organization at large (Holmes and Hawood 2023). The theory also applies to crisis communication and conflict resolution with hostile publics, by finding ways to demonstrate at least some area of common identity to mitigate hostility (e.g., Yook and Stacks 2024). Showing appreciation and rewarding interaction to bolster social identity with a group lays the groundwork for positive future communication in that group.

Symbolic Convergence Theory

Much of communication theory is about understanding how people determine meaning. The idea that group members share consciousness and meaning as they interact with one another is the essence of *symbolic convergence theory*. A key concept in this theory is "fantasy themes," which are a way of understanding the meaning of events that fulfills a rhetorical or psychological need. Meaning is influenced by what one wants to communicate or think (Bormann 1982).

Fantasy themes can be seen in the way a person might dramatize a message with a joke, innuendo, pun, or anecdote. The themes are built on and embellished in fantasy chains through group interactions. Different group members contribute to the fantasy theme in their own way, which leads to group cohesion—this is called symbolic convergence, from which the theory gets its name.

Fantasy themes are made more likely in groups when they are given ambiguous instruction, input, or evaluation. For example, a client or boss expressing minimal satisfaction with a group's work could be taken to mean the group did not perform well, or it could be interpreted to mean the client or boss did not appreciate the hard work or creative professionalism of the group. In other words, lack of clear communication to a group allows group members to specify the meaning that matches their fantasy theme.

Professionals can apply this theory to themselves and try to be careful of making meaning match a desire, as opposed to seeking an objective understanding. Professionals should also understand that groups—and their members—to whom they communicate may not understand an intended meaning but instead read or hear what they want based on a psychological need or a message they want to convey. Such misinterpretation of meaning can be avoided not only with clarity in messaging but by understanding the communicative and psychological needs of audience groups and appealing to those needs. Professionals should strategically offset an ability to reinterpret a meaning or make messages too clear to be subjectively interpreted.

CHAPTER 4

Organizational Theories

The work of public relations professionals is centered on organizations. In Part 6, the concept of organization–public relationships (OPRs) will be addressed. This chapter will look generally at theories about organizational communication, recognizing that there is public relations activity within organizations, and on behalf of organizations to external publics and other organizations. Organization theory has obvious value in this context.

Systems Theory

A system is a common word but when applied specifically to theory, can be considered a set of interrelated parts that create a unique, bonded entity (organization) (Thayer, 1968, 1987; Witmer 2006) or "a set of objects or entities that interrelate with one another to form a whole" (Littlejohn 1989, 35).

There are four parts of a system according to *systems theory*: objects, or the individual parts and members of a system; the attributes of the system; the internal relationships among members of the system; and the surrounding environment. Organizations are said to be "cybernetic" or sensitive to their environment (Witmer 2006), although organizations can be open or closed to their environment. Cybernetics, related to systems theory, is the study of the regulation and control of systems with an emphasis on feedback (Littlejohn 1989).

It is easy to see the connection of public relations practice to systems theory. Public relations professionals communicate with various publics within *and* external to organizations and should be naturally inclined to think systemically, even if unaware of the theory. But being mindful of the theory makes practice more intentional and strategic. Public relations as an organizational function is both a system component and a boundary spanner, meaning a communication liaison between and among the various "objects" in the system (Witmer 2006). In systems theory, public relations activities serve as a feedback function, although the profession also enables the interactions and interrelations that define a system in the first place.

That said, systems theory is also limited with regard to public relations application. It is time bound, discounts the recursive nature of communication, and does not consider the creation of publics through shared experiences. Because of these limitations, systems theory does not adequately facilitate the creation of culture within organizations (Witmer 2006).

Systems theory is related to the *theory of structuration*, also called *structuration theory* (Kolasi 2020; Giddens 1984). While systems theory focuses on how various parts relate to each other, structuration theory takes a broader view and advocates looking both at structures and practice, because social structures or systems are formed by and through human interactions. For public relations professionals, this would mean thinking about how an organization's interface with its environment contributes to broader social structures, how publics are conversational communities that move from topic to topic, and how organizational culture is based on lived experiences and not just a response to messages and slogans. Professionals, therefore, should not assume they can communicate in isolation. Practice should be, to borrow a common strategic expression, like playing chess instead of checkers to see the whole board and plan moves and anticipate reactions.

Conversational Human Voice

In a professional world, where organizations are increasingly expected to "take a stand on social issues," or even just be responsive to its various publics, the issue is not whether they are communicative but *how*. *Conversational human voice* (CHV) is a concept more than a theory and relates to the tone or the voice of a message as being as important as or more important than the content in terms of public perception and response. "Conversational human voice describes an engaging and natural style of organizational communication as perceived by an organization's publics based on interactions between individuals in the organization and individuals in publics" (Kelleher 2009, 177).

CHV has been found in blog interactions to correlate with all four factors in the way relationships are measured: public reported levels of trust, satisfaction, commitment, and control mutuality with the organization (Hon and Grunig 1999). Another study centered on social media interactions found that public perception of organizational reputation was higher when communication exhibited CHV as compared with an institutional voice and when the tone was concrete as opposed to abstract (Huang and Ki 2023). This study led to a model that states that construal level (concrete or abstract) combined with CHV led to a positive perception of an organization's social presence and perceived organizational listening, which in turn led to a positive organizational reputation. *Social presence* is defined as the perception of an authentic response to social media complaints. *Organizational listening* is demonstrated by an organization demonstrating efforts to understand, acknowledge, and respond appropriately. Reputation is defined as how well an organization meets expectations.

These studies, and the concept of CHV, should inform professionals charged with crafting message and message strategies to consider not just content but also *style* and *tone*. This is important whether the message comes from the public relations professional, a CEO, or generically from the organization. Using words that indicate genuine human emotion, concern, anticipation, and other conversational language is more effective than simply crafted announcements for building and maintaining relationships and reputation.

Speech Act Theory

Speech act theory is part of the philosophy of language that looks at language processes, how expressions acquire meaning, and is therefore a theory of communication. The theory has been applied in economics, sociology, and artificial intelligence (AI). It has a grounding in ontology, or a branch of philosophy centered on the state of being or a set of rules or facts. It is related to organizations and public relations because of its examination of public statements.

Basically, statements or expressions can be constative, or descriptive statements of fact, or they can be performative expressions used to promise or complete actions—hence the term "speech act." Performative statements can be propositional and describe an action, elocutionary speaking, or writing that constitutes the act itself, or perlocution, which is speaking or writing that has an action as an aim but does not affect the action. There are five specific types of performative statements:

1. Assertives—statements or descriptions that respect how things are;
2. Directives—orders or commands to get hearers or readers to act;
3. Commissives—promises, pledges, or vows that the speaker will act;
4. Expressions—apology, thanks, congratulations that share an attitude; and
5. Declarations—statements that are the act itself—e.g., "I resign" or "you are fired." (Mobaquiao 2018)

The application of this theory is to acknowledge there is a difference between what is promised and what is done. Publics can discern when a statement is merely what an organization says it will do as compared to a track record of consistent action. Public relations professionals should speak and write being conscious of whether they are promising or delivering—is the speech an action itself or merely promising one? The response of an audience could be dependent on the difference in terms of whether they believe the message, change their attitude, or enact a positive behavior of their own. As such, speech act theory has direct strategic implications for reputation management.

Balance Theory

Experienced public relations professionals who communicate on behalf of an organization to many other publics with competing interests know the importance of balance. *Balance theory* is based on the premise that people prefer relationships that maintain balanced states of agreement and harmony. While the focus is on interpersonal relationships, the theory is applicable to attitudes and opinions about causes, events, brands, and ideas and is therefore practically relevant to organizational communication as well.

Balance theory can be visualized as a triangle of relationships between a person or organization, another person or public, and an element of comparison such as an opinion or idea (Heider 1946). The relationships between each pair (dyad) in the triangle can be positive or negative. The two persons (or organization and public) can be positive in terms of similarities or sentiment toward the other. The relationship between the persons (organization, public) and the object can be positive if the opinion is the same as their own or they support the idea.

The important aspect of the theory is balance. In the triangle, there is balance if all three relationships are positive or one is positive and two are negative. There is imbalance whenever there is an odd number of negative relationships, either one or three. A way to understand this simply is with the statements "my friend's friend is my friend" (three positive relationships with overall balance) or "my friend's enemy is my enemy" (two negative and one positive relationship are also balanced). In the latter case, a person and friend bond and have balance in their mutual dislike of some enemy. Another view of balance is to see an organization and a key public sharing a negative view of proposed legislation. But if an organization is in favor (positive) of the legislation and the public is not (negative) and if the organization and public have a positive existing relationship, there is imbalance.

In states of imbalance, people will seek balance. Organizations may do the same. This can be done by ignoring issues or focusing on different ones. It can also mean breaking off or diminishing a relationship and elevating others. This is relevant in public relations with modern concern for corporate social advocacy (CSA) (discussed specifically in Part 5) on issues and how to appeal to segmented publics regarding ideas and opinions based on current relationship and public opinion and sentiment on ideas and issues. Professionals should know when initially engaging a public whether they are entering into a balanced or unbalanced situation. If the latter, seeking balance should precede sending messages focused only on achieving organizational goals.

CHAPTER 5

Intercultural Communication Theory

The broadest scope for communication theory goes beyond interpersonal, small group, and organizational focus to address cultures. A culture has been defined as "a system of meanings shared and continuously created among a specific group of people" (Sha et al. 2018, 72). Other scholars have considered cultures to be based on norms that guide behavior. A distinction can be made between cross-cultural communication, which is "comparison and contrasting communication phenomenon across different cultures," and intercultural communications, which has to do with the "study of social interactions between or among culturally dissimilar individuals or groups" (Sha et al. 2018, 73).

It should be noted that cultures can be viewed in terms of organizations, nations, races, and other ways people group themselves together. So while intercultural communication is of obvious interest to public relations professionals working for an MNC (multinational corporation) or NGO (nongovernmental organization), it is also directly useful to anyone working domestically with a variety of ethnic groups or other groups of people with distinct cultures different than others.

Hofstede's Cultural Dimensions

Because national cultures vary so much and in complex ways, Geert Hofstede sought to codify the differences between cultures in a small set of scales or dimensions of culture. He did this by conducting a survey of 116,000 IBM employees in 40 countries. This data led to the development of *Hofstede's Global Cultural Dimension Index* (Roy 2020).

The five dimensions of culture Hofstede determined are scales. In other words, they are not one or the other, but a country or culture would be at some point between the two extremes. These dimensions include the following:

- Individualism–Collectivism. Individualism equates with independence and valuing uniqueness and achievement. Collective cultures place the group before the individual in terms of value and duty and stress cooperation over competition.
- High–Low Uncertainty Avoidance. Cultures with high uncertainty avoidance value blunt expression, rules, and precision. A low uncertainty avoidance culture may be more innovative and considers ambiguity necessary for communication to allow others more ability to interpret meaning.
- Power Distance. Cultures with high levels of power distance consider inequity normal and acceptable. Low levels of power distance are in cultures where people do not assume that people higher up in a hierarchy are superior.
- Masculinity–Femininity. This dimension has to do with the degree of defined emotional roles for men and women. Masculine cultures have more such definition of roles and feminine cultures have fewer.
- Long–Short-Term Orientation. Short-term orientation is evidence by cultures that focus on the present, whereas a long-term orientation would be seen in cultures that revere the past and that are mindful of their impact on the future (Hofstede 1980; Hofstede and Hofstede 1980).

Another scholar contributed the dimension of high–low context. This has to do with whether a meaning is derived from contextual cues (high context) rather than primarily from the words themselves (low context) (Hall 1976). Contextual cues include the location of interaction, the status of the people involved, whether the communication is interpersonal or in a group, and other factors.

Professionals communicating within or to different cultures can strategically frame messages according to recipient public and stakeholder culture and where they fall on these dimensions. It is important to resonate positively and not offend or be misunderstood due to cultural variables. For example, stressing a product's appeal to individuality may work in the United States, which tends toward an individualistic culture, but not in Japan, which is more collectivist and even has a cultural expression, "the nail that sticks up gets hammered down." Considering where a public of interest is on the other dimensions prior to communicating could contribute significantly to strategy. The most relevant dimensions depend on the goal and topic of communication in specific situations.

Cultural Value Orientation Theory

Similarly to Hofstede's cultural dimensions, *cultural value orientation theory* lists seven cultural value orientations that form three dimensions on bipolar scales. The values and scales were developed from data in 76 national cultures and seven transnational cultural groups (Schwartz 2006). The seven cultural value orientations are as follows:

1. Harmony—unity with nature, seeks peace in the world;
2. Embeddedness—characterized by desire for social order, obedience, respect for tradition;
3. Hierarchy—respect for authority, humble;
4. Mastery—a form of ambition or daring;
5. Affective autonomy—seeking pleasure, free pursuit of personal desire;
6. Intellectual autonomy—considered to be curious and broad-minded; and
7. Egalitarianism—values social justice, equality.

The values toward which a culture is oriented, in general, serve to guide the behaviors of individuals in that culture. These prevailing values also guide individual attitudes and public opinion at large. The three-dimensional scales derived from these values are as follows:

1. People are autonomous versus embedded in their groups.
   This would mean that either emotional and intellectual autonomy would be of high value or that embeddedness or group loyalty would prevail.

2. Egalitarian versus hierarchical. Where a culture lands on a scale between these two value orientations is indicative of how much people care about and work to preserve social fabric.

3. Harmony versus mastery. How people manage these two values affects their relationship to the natural and social world around them (Schwartz 2006).

Another way of considering how cultural values differ is through a series of five questions (Kluckolm and Stratbeck 1961). The questions are as follows:

1. What is human nature? (good, evil, a mixture);
2. What is the relationship between humans, nature, and the supernatural? (Domination, submissive, supernatural);
3. What is the concept of time, and where is the focus? (past, present, future);
4. What motivates human behavior? (self-expression, personal growth, obtain power); and
5. What is the nature of human relations? (hierarchy, equality) (Kluckolm and Stratbeck 1961).

There are many ways cultures and individuals vary, but these questions, values, and dimension scales indicate a common worldview and set of cultural values. These typologies make understanding cultural differences simpler and lend themselves to specific strategies. Considering these can be useful for public relations professionals in different cultural contexts to plan campaign and message strategy and predict collective response in terms of attitude and behavior.

Cross-Cultural Adaptation Theory

How or whether people assimilate to other cultures is important for professionals to consider for several reasons. For one, they themselves may need to work in another culture. Second, developing lasting relationships with individuals and publics in other cultures will require sensitivity to the influences and barriers to people adapting to the professional's culture. This cannot be assumed and should be strategically and appropriately fostered by public relations professionals working in international companies, nonprofit organizations, or for government entities.

Cross-cultural adaptation theory is useful by spelling out another typology. There are five structural features that influence adapting to another culture:

1. The predisposition of the "sojourner" (person traveling across cultures for a short- or long-term period). How open are they to adapting?
2. The host environment. How receptive to strangers is the country or organization within another culture?
3. Personal communication. How competent is the sojourner in communicating within the host culture?
4. Social communication. The level of engagement in host culture interpersonal and mediated communication; and
5. Identity transformation. This relates to psychological health, intercultural identity, and functional fitness. It is somewhat related to "culture shock." The more a person sees themselves with a dual identity (relating to both their home and the other culture), the more likely they can adapt (Kim 2001).

Going into a new culture has been compared to an organism going into a new habitat. The goal of adaptation is to reach a new equilibrium in a new environment, such as comfort and efficiency of communication (Kim 2005). The process of adapting to communicate in a new culture follows a series of steps or phenomena. The first is *deviation*, in which a communication encounter is interpreted as different than the home culture, either verbally or nonverbally. This creates a stressor of psychological uncertainty or confusion. To overcome this stressor, a person acculturates their communication by adopting elements of the host culture. This is followed by or simultaneous with *deculturation*—or letting go of some elements or biases of communication from the home culture. The process results in a person being intercultural in their communication and even identity (Kim 2005).

Considering again that a culture could be a country, race, organization, or any way people are bonded to each other, the public relations professional who has knowledge of these features can apply them to themselves to be intentional in adapting to another culture. Or they can encourage another individual or group to adapt to their culture by strategically being welcoming, encouraging communication, and acknowledging their home identity along with their presence in another culture.

Cultural Identity Theory

Identity in a cultural context is addressed by *cultural identity theory*. The theory describes the process of people forming a cultural identity through social interactions. There cultural identities have seven properties:

1. Cultural identity is formed when a person shows patterns of behavior that are influenced by multiple cultural groups they belong to or endorse. These groups can be racial, national, gender, ideology, religion, and others.
2. A person perceives a different degree of relevance of their cultural identity based on the communication milieu.
3. Cultural identities vary in terms of how widely held they are by others in the same culture and therefore generalization should be done carefully.
4. Identities can be developed by "arousal" or self-conception as well as by "ascription," meaning an identity is imposed on one by others.
5. Cultural identities vary in how much they are acted on, or the intensity of the identity.
6. Cultural identities have many elements that can be stable or change over time.
7. There are both content (topic) and relational (communicator) aspects to cultural identities being acted on (Collier and Thomas 1988; Sha et al. 2018).

This list of characteristics of cultural identities is complex given that they change over time and are considered by individuals to be based to varying degrees on context. But professionals can still employ these strategically by considering aspects of cultural identity when communicating cross culturally each time, whether these cultural identities based on these factors would affect a message being attended to, received, perceived as appropriate and relevant, and ultimately lead to a reason to change opinion or action. Communicating with, not to or about, a cultural identity is the strategic path to good and effective communication.

Expectancy Violation Theory

Another way of thinking about cultural adaptation is how expectations for routine communication are not met when communicating cross culturally. This is the essence of *expectancy violation theory*, in which an individual's evaluation of a communication interaction is based on factors related to the communicator, the context, and the relationship (Burgoon 1993). The positive or negative outcome of communication is dependent on the degree to which someone's expectations for communication are fulfilled or violated. Expectancy is about an enduring pattern of communication, not just a single interaction, and can be particular to an individual or general to a group. This makes it essential for a public relations professional to know what a public in another culture would expect of communication interpersonally and organizationally.

Understanding the concepts within this theory make it even more relevant. A communication expectancy means communication behavior observed in the past is anticipated again. Expectancy violation means the public or individual perceives that current communication is not consistent with past patterns. The receiver then does an appraisal process to determine the meaning of the violation. A behavior violation valence means the violation can be seen as negative or positive. A negative expectancy violation may be attributed to incompetence, ignorance, or disrespect. An expectancy exceeded positively is seen to be clear, relevant, and competent. The effects of violation as addressed in the theory can be seen in an immediate communication response, the communication outcomes, or relational outcomes (Burgoon and Hubbard 2005). The response could be negative to the point where a crisis develops, a campaign fails, or organizational reputation could suffer. Each of these concepts and outcomes can be considered as culturally driven (Sha et al. 2018).

A public relations professional can apply this theory strategically by considering each of the factors. As for the communicator, or messenger, the professional should consider who speaks or writes given their personality, appearance, and communication style. The relational factor can be viewed in terms of long- or short-term relationship, similarities, familiarity, and whether status is equal or not. Paying attention to the context of communication is also important, such as whether it is a private or open setting or an informal or formal setting and whether the communication is task-focused or relational in orientation. These factors should guide a professional's decision about what is communicated and how in order to meet public relations goals.

Strategic Summary of Part II— Communication

The notion that a communicator should know their audience is fundamental. The communication theories in this part introduce a variety of concepts and propositions about audiences that help a professional to think more strategically about understanding and approaching audiences or publics.

- Public relations theory makes a distinction between audiences, publics, and stakeholders. Audiences passively receive messages; publics have a relationship with an issue; stakeholders have a relationship with the organization.
- The communication process can be seen in terms of mathematics or engineering. Paying attention to the entire process, including "noise" or interference in the process, is vital to making sure messages are properly understood.
- People derive much meaning in communication by interpretation of symbols, not just literal words.
- Communication interactions are defined by the exchanges that happen in relationships, and people weigh the costs and benefits to themselves of being in those relationships.

- People try to resolve uncertainty before paying attention to messages, so communicators should strategically work to reduce uncertainty in the relationship first and then deliver the intended message.
- Nonverbal communication can have as much impact if not more on gaining attention and understanding as verbal communication.
- People interpret messages on whether the communicator is trying to dominate or control the relationship and the degree to which they appreciate or affiliate with the communicator. Building relationships before communicating is a wise strategy.
- If people see a power imbalance in a relationship in terms of dependency, they may be reluctant to communicate with an organization and may seek alternative relationships.
- Using a strategic group process can prevent groupthink— people in a group valuing consensus over critical thinking— and leads to better group decision making and outcomes.
- Group membership can be a significant part of someone's social identity and can affect how they interpret communication to themselves and/or the group.
- People may construct their own view of reality, called "fantasy themes," and use that to make meaning of ambiguous messages.
- Communication does not happen in isolation but is part of a broader system, and people view individual messages as part of that broader experienced context.
- Organizations that communicate with a conversational voice can enhance their relationships with publics, increasing attention and reputation.
- Much communication is seen not merely as words but as a performance, and audiences discern if messages are descriptions, commands, promises, expression of attitude, or statements of intended action.
- If a public senses an imbalance between themselves and an organization regarding agreement on a topic, they are less likely to attend to the message.

- Different aspects of cultural values affect how people understand and interpret messages.
- If a person's expectation for a relationship is not met over time, they leave that relationship and/or no longer pay attention to messages.

PART III

Media Theories—Making Smart Channel Choices

When public relations professionals are planning a campaign or choosing a response to a public, they must choose the tactics or channels they will use to reach selected publics. This chapter covers a range of media theories that can help add strategy or realistic expectations to that choice.

"Media" often connotes news media, and this chapter starts with some older but still relevant theories about the news media. But in its literal sense, it means a medium between two parties, or a channel of communications. Already a century ago, shortly after the field went from being called press agentry to publicity to public relations, early pioneers like Edward Bernays, Ivy Lee, and Arthur Page were insisting they did far more than send news releases in their public relations work (Penning 2008).

For years, public relations professionals have advocated using a "media mix" of traditional publicity and purchasing advertising and creating a variety of media produced by the organization. These have been conceptualized as controlled and uncontrolled and have more recently been described as a PESO model for paid, earned, shared, and owned media (Dietrich 2024).

This chapter reviews media theories starting with historical, one-way theories specifically about the news media. While these are old, they are relevant because they are foundational and show how theory and the public relations profession developed alongside changes in media. They also have practical application even today, although in a different media environment. A second set of theories addresses how the public responds to media, also called media effects theories. Finally, there is a section of recent theory addressing digital media.

CHAPTER 6

Foundational One-Way News Media Theories

In the early 1900s, when the profession was new as a full-time occupation, those who practiced what eventually became known as public relations were called *press agents* or *publicity men*. Their emphasis then—and unfortunately the limited public understanding of the public relations profession today—was on getting information to the public via the news media, which at the time was entirely print. The theory that emerged at that time was therefore focused on the process that occurred between public relations practitioners and journalists and that resulted in news and publicity.

Agenda-Setting Theory

In the 1920s, with an explosive growth in the economy, media consumption, and the profession of public relations, much attention was given to the concept of public opinion, with more than 20 books written on the subject in that decade (Penning 2008). Journalist Walter Lippman wrote one of those books and laid the groundwork for agenda-setting theory when he noted that the media have the potential to structure issues for the public (Lippmann 1989). He also made clear that the media can influence what people talk about but not exactly what to think. He described all of this as a pseudo-environment of pictures in our heads created by the media that we respond to. The media can do this according to Lippman because they "choose and display news" (Lippmann 1989, 5).

A formal theory called *agenda setting* developed years later, when scholars asked whether the media reflects society or society reflects what is in the news media. (McCombs and Shaw 1972). The proposed theory defined "agenda" as the events or topics the public should consider important and discuss but also stressed that the public determines what they think about those topics (i.e., opinion), consistent with Lippmann's original assertion.

Later, the theory was extended. The original was called "first-level" agenda setting, to which was added the concept of "second-level" agenda setting. While first-level puts a topic on the public agenda, so to speak, second-level agenda-setting frames that topic in terms of how it is covered—the angle, the tone, and the details included and excluded (McCombs and Evatt 1995; Ghanem 1997). This extension of the theory is relevant today, with a polarized media leading to a polarized public with what some see as bias in what is and is not covered and how news topics are framed. Public relations professionals increasingly have to consider not only whether the topic is relevant to a journalist's beat or media outlet's topical focus but also the pattern of ideological subjectivity and how they may frame the news being pitched.

At the 50th anniversary of the agenda-setting theory, the original author reflected on the theory in light of the current media and cultural environment and, in 2014, wrote an article with collaborators extending the theory yet again (McCombs et al. 2014). Their reimagined theory is more complex and has a third level and a total of seven facets:

1. The basic or first-level agenda setting is about the relevance of issues, political figures, and other objects of attention.
2. The second level is about the relevance of the attributes of these objects or subjects.
3. A new third-level agenda setting is about a networked media agenda and its impact on a networked public agenda. Neither the media nor any individual exists or communicates in isolation. "In reality objects and their attributes are bundled together in media messages and in public thought and conversation" (McCombs et al. 2014, 792).
4. The fourth facet introduces several new concepts to the theory. Each individual has a need for orientation, or a psychological need to be familiar with surroundings, to fill in detail, and to intellectually know where they are going. People pay attention to media

due to a combination of finding something relevant but having uncertainty about it. If an individual has a high need for orientation, they will seek "vertical" media (mainstream) and be affected by first-level agenda setting. If they have a moderate need for orientation, they will seek "horizontal" (niche) media and be affected by second-level agenda setting.

5. Consequences of agenda setting has effects at all three levels for attitudes, opinions, and behavior of members of the public.

6. The origins of the media agenda are varied. They include the cultural and ideological environment, news sources, how the media influence each other, journalism and industry norms, and the characteristics of individual journalists.

7. "Agendamelding" is another new concept in the refashioned agenda-setting theory. The authors describe it as "the way we merge the civic agendas of the media and our valued reference communities with our personal views and experiences to create a satisfying picture of the world" (McCombs et al. 2014, 782).

This expanded theory and specific facets reveal how bias enters into news via market pressure on news corporations, as well as from the values, experiences, and perspectives of individual reporters and editors. Therefore, public relations professionals need to consider subjective factors as much as news value when pitching news ideas to journalists.

Whereas the original agenda-setting theory focused on the news media, the updated theory can be applied by public relations professionals to all forms of media, including social media, bloggers, podcasters, and the like. Public relations professionals could never expect that getting information into the media would necessarily change opinions and behaviors, and that is especially true now. There is great competition for attention in all forms of media, and with its competing perspectives. The concept of "agenda melding" also presents a caution and an opportunity for public relations professionals who are now direct players and sometimes competitors with the news media to set the agenda of topics for the public. As the authors note, "with the widespread diffusion of social media, agenda-setting can be applied to a much wider array of channels and more easily to an array of content extending far beyond the traditional focus on public affairs" (McCombs et al. 2014, 788). That means the public relations industry can participate in setting the public agenda directly as well as indirectly.

Gatekeeping Theory

The concept of gatekeeping exists in the theory of several fields. With regard to communication and media, it emerged when a Boston University professor wrote a case study of how an Associated Press wire editor determined which stories were rejected and which put forward on the wire (White 1950). He found that the editor in this case was influenced by their own subjective experiences, attitudes, and expectations.

That initial research led to much more on the subject and eventually emerged as *gatekeeping theory*. The essence of it is that journalists engage in a process of reviewing countless bits of information and culling them into the limited number of messages that reach people each day, which is a significant role in society (Shoemaker and Vos 2009).

As with agenda-setting theory, the older gatekeeping theory has been updated. A study looked at Silicon Valley tech platforms (i.e., social media) as a new framework and an elaboration of the notion of gatekeeping information in public life (Vos and Russell 2019). The idea is that other social institutions, in addition to journalism, shape news too and that these range from government to the profession of public relations. Journalists determine what gets through the gate into their news outlets, but these other institutions put pressure on journalists. The pressure could be in the form of market forces, advertisers, audiences, sources, and technology. Some of that pressure recently could be competition in the form of organizations using their own blogs, podcasts, websites, direct mail, and other tactics to reach the public apart from the news media. "These institutional forces seem to work in a greater variety of ways than gatekeeping theory has heretofore acknowledged" (Vos and Russell 2019, 23–34). An additional factor is that algorithms automate some of the gatekeeping through a computer-mediated set of instructions to identify and determine utility. Also, news is not a single story but an ongoing process and conversation that journalists have with audiences online.

This broader view of gatekeeping has numerous applications for public relations professionals. One is to understand the pressures on journalists and use that information strategically in media relations when trying to get information into the media. Another is to consider those alternative media where the gate may be more open. A third is to take the role of gatekeeper as public relations professionals seriously and use owned and shared media to let information flow through numerous gates to a series of smaller but fertile pastures beyond in the form of niche publics who are seeking the information being shared.

Cultivation Theory

It was a study about violence on television and its impact on the public that led to *cultivation theory* (Gerbner et al. 1980). More than 500 articles on the theory were published by 2014 (Potter 2014). The term *cultivation* is a metaphor from agriculture, in which the repeated plowing of a field in the same direction leads to neat rows for seeding, growth, and harvesting crops. With regard to media, cultivation theory "predicts that the amount of time spent watching TV influences viewers' perception of reality due to repeated exposure to common themes" (Dainton and Zelley 2023). The theory is concerned with patterns of communication on television occurring over time and not single episodes or specific content (Gerbner et al. 1986). The idea is that television homogenizes culture as a mass medium. However, different groups are affected differently based on how much television they watch, what they watch, and their existing knowledge and opinion. Someone uninformed on a given topic who sees repeated messages on that topic presented in the same way or with the same perspective is most susceptible to their understanding of that topic being cultivated by media exposure.

Testing of the theory over time has shown weak support. Today, media message production is fragmented among many media channels, and people selectively expose themselves to different media and messages (Potter 2014). However, cultivation still happens, albeit differently.

Of relevance to public relations professionals is that cultivation theory has shown to be a reality, with branding messages on blogs and social media cultivating consumer attitudes toward brands (Potter 2014).

One such study of cultivation by brands resulted in four implications for public relations practice:

1. The quality of exposure is more important than the quantity of exposure. Professionals should push the right information over time that is both consistent with corporate objectives and interesting and engaging to consumers;
2. Professionals should "think global and act local" by satisfying followers' interests around their homes, adapting messages and topics to a given geographic region;
3. Brands should interact with followers and engage in dialogue and show respect; and
4. The messaging to cultivate attitudes should be done by professionals skilled in communication, problem solving, and analytical and technology skills as well as trained in ways to interact and spark interest (Wei et al. 2020).

Again, while the theory started out to indicate public relations professionals needed to encourage cultivation by journalists, now they can do so themselves. They can use multiple forms of media to do so, but they should do so with strategy.

Media Dependency Theory

Sometimes the only way people can know something is if someone tells them. That is the basis of *media dependency theory*, which states that "audiences depend on media information to meet needs and obtain goals" (Littlejohn 1989, 278). The theory assumes a three-way interaction among media, their audiences, and society at large.

Even though the news media has changed and there is a proliferation of information online currently, audiences are still dependent on modern forms of media varying by circumstances. The greater the need someone has for information, the stronger their dependency on media of some form and the more likely that the information supplied will alter their awareness, feelings, and behaviors (Ball-Rokeach and DeFleur 1976). The theory evolved with time and media changes. Media technology does not negate the dependency on media but means the media—understood broadly—take on more unique information functions. A model developed to illustrate media dependency theory shows reciprocal relationships between social systems (whose stability varies), media systems (whose centrality of information varies), and audiences (whose dependency varies). Social systems and media systems influence each other, and both in turn influence audiences. Audiences are affected cognitively, affectively (emotionally), and behaviorally. The effects in the audience then affect the social systems and media systems in the reciprocal relationships. To summarize the model:

> when media messages are not linked to audience dependencies and when people's social realities are entirely adequate before and during message reception, media messages may have little or no alteration effects. They may reinforce existing beliefs or behavior forms. In contrast, when people do not have social realities that provide adequate frameworks for understanding, acting and escaping, and when audiences are dependent in these ways on media information received, such messages may have a number of alternative effects … in terms of cognition, affective and/or overt activity (Ball-Rokeach and DeFleur 1976, 19).

Even though the theory has progressed, so has the legacy media, and they are still relevant in terms of audience dependency. One study of tweets during a crisis situation showed that the legacy media are major sources of information for social media users, who engage media content within social platforms (Jin and Spence 2023). Legacy media have their own social feeds and the exchange information with social media. In the study, 7 of 20 influencers were news organizations, and 70 percent of the top domains of URLs linked in posts related to the crisis tracked to news media outlets. So public relations professionals should not entirely abandon legacy media but engage them in new ways, recognizing the dependency that organizations and their audiences may have on media. Public relations professionals can also respond to that dependency by providing information, with the organizations they represent being part of the social institutions involved in reciprocal relationships with media and audiences.

Public Sphere

The *public sphere* is not really a news media theory but a good bridge to the next category of theory. A concept born of critical theory, the public sphere is a construct of information sharing that exists between civil society and the state. State authority is monitored and kept in check by informed and critical discourse of the people (Habermas 1984). The sphere arose thanks to the rise of the novel and literacy, an increase in political journalism, and the robust discussions that happened in coffee houses.

True to form for critical theory, Habermas saw flaws in how the public sphere changed conceptually from a liberal public sphere of citizen dialogue to a market-driven public sphere characterized by governments and organizations expressing competing interests and actually excluding the public. He spoke with disdain of public opinion research, publicity, and public relations work (Habermas 1991).

Public relations professionals could object to a negative characterization of the profession, or they could work to practice in a way that does not merit Habermas' criticism. Contemporary scholars have considered the criticism of the public sphere and identified four phenomena related to the digital era. Professionals could consider these and practice in a way that addresses these new realities to encourage a public sphere that is closer to the ideal of empowering the public to engage in civil dialogue. The phenomena identified are as follows:

1. Digital platforms are the organizing principle of digital communications and neglect the responsibility for civic exchanges;
2. A shift in media consumption means less reading, attention, and depth;
3. Surveillance capitalism and algorithmic personalization deteriorates an inclusive public sphere, manipulates the online environment, and primes people for divisiveness; and
4. What was public is now a new intimate public sphere that erodes the distinction between public and private, where identities are emotional and not rational (Staab and Thiel 2022).

CHAPTER 7

Media Effects Theories

The first set of theories in Part III were about how and why people pay attention to the media and what public relations professionals can think about as they try to reach mass audiences. This section describes theories that go further than awareness and the media ecosystem to speak more to the effects of the media on people's understanding, attitude, opinion, and behavior. Since public relations professionals today seek more than just a number of clips or media "hits" and estimated awareness, these theories will lend even more to strategic consideration of desired public response. When discussing outcomes and change in attitude and behavior, persuasion is necessary. That will be the focus of Part IV. For now, it is important to understand the baseline of how media can be part of the influence on opinion and action.

Framing Theory

Imagine a picture that needs to be framed. Placing a smaller frame on a larger picture involves necessarily leaving some of the picture out of view of what is in the frame. That is the essence of *framing theory*.

Building on agenda-setting theory, particularly its second level, framing theory focuses on the essence of the issues at hand rather than a specific topic. A frame in this theory is what aspects are emphasized and consequently what other aspects are ignored (Goffman 1974). People interpret their world through a personal framework. The media influences this with the way they frame news stories, which are abstractions that structure and organize meaning and thus influence the perception of news by the audience. There are two distinctions or types of frameworks: (1) natural frameworks are things that happen naturally or literally, and (2) social frameworks are built on natural frameworks but are driven by the whims and manipulations of other people. It could be considered as the distinction between objective and subjective (biased) reporting.

The theory was refined with a typology of seven specific framing techniques (Fairhurst and Sarr 1996):

1. Metaphor, or comparison;
2. Stories, such as myths, legends, and narratives;
3. Traditions, including cultural rituals and ceremonies;
4. Slogans that are used to be memorable;
5. Artifacts that have symbolic value;
6. Contrast, describing what something is not; and
7. Spin, create intended positive or negative bias.

A further extension of this theory was the development of a process model of framing. The model recognizes that there are media frames and individual frames in society that are in conflict, compatible, or created (the media initiates a frame in a public not engaged or knowledgeable of an issue). Media frames in this model have an impact on the public but also result from influences on the media (Scheufele 1999).

In the model, journalists respond to inputs that include pressure from their corporate media environment, their own ideological attitudes, and other social elites. Journalists are also audiences of the publics' attitudes and behaviors. The output of all of these inputs is the media frame. The process then moves to the audience, which takes their own framework and the media frame, either adapts the media frame or reinforces their own, and the outcome is attribution of responsibility for the frame and their changed or consistent attitudes and behaviors related to the topic (Scheufele 1999).

The application of framing for public relations professionals is two-fold. First, they must be conscious of the media's framing, often called *narrative*, which varies by topic and from one journalist or media corporation to another. Second, public relations professionals can be mindful of how they are framing, intentionally or not, and seek to do so strategically and ethically. The public relations profession is often accused of "spin," which is one technique on the typology of framing and connotes deceit and manipulation. But framing can also be ethical and consistent with the profession when it is about advocacy. Good public relations professionals have been doing this for years, not just in media relations but in everything from advertising slogans to speechwriting. Examples of doing so would be to say or write "this is what is most important" or "here is the way to think about this." This is advocating a point of view and is consistent with a public relations professional's duty to the organization they represent. So long as framing is transparent it is not unethical (more on that subject in Part V). Given the foregoing model, based on research, it is also strategic to weigh the fact that publics have existing frameworks for which a public relations frame may be consistent or contradictory. Strategy and objective change is based on which framework is in the mind of the intended public, so research should be done to discover that before communication.

Social Learning Theory

Social learning theory (Bandura 1977) is a social-psychological theory that focuses on human learning in social environments. The theory is a bridge between a behavioral and cognitive approach in its consideration of the relationship between a learning environment and cognitive behavior in influencing learning behavior. It is relevant to public relations practice because public relations campaigns have the objective, whether stated in these terms or not, to affect the learning of intended publics—about an event, a brand, a product, a cause, an election—and to change attitudes and behaviors relative to the focus of a campaign. For example, five specific measures in what is called the B.A.S.I.C. model have been proposed to determine whether a public relations program or campaign is having a behavioral impact on intended publics. Through interviews with samples from the target publics about a company brand, product, or issue, professionals can learn if the public has a desired: (1) awareness; (2) accurate knowledge; (3) a perception that messages are relevant to them; (4) intent to take promoted action; and (5) a willingness to advocate for the company, brand, product, or issue based on their experience (Michaelson and Stacks 2011).

Social learning theory starts with the assumption that humans are active information processors. Individuals can learn by creating a conducive learning environment, engaging in continuous observation, or self-directed learning. The social aspect of the theory is the proposition that people often learn new behaviors by observing and imitating others. They acquire knowledge, beliefs, skills, attitudes, and behaviors by watching the actions of others and observing the positive or negative consequences that follow. A form of equation to simply illustrate social learning theory is {environment + cognitive factors = learning and behavior}. A process model would include attention, followed by retention, leading to motor reproduction (perform observed behavior), resulting in motivation or will to continue. It is a precursor and is similar to some common adoption models in marketing and public relations, such as the sales funnel or the steps to adopt an opinion or purchase a product.

The theory includes three models of observational learning that could be the key applications for public relations professionals. Strategies and tactics could incorporate one or all of these models to encourage publics to learn whatever specific behavior is in the campaign objectives:

1. *Live*—observe actual person. Consider testimonials and influencers.
2. *Verbal instruction and description.* This is where good writing skills apply.
3. *Symbolic*—through media, books, videos, and so on. Demonstrate desired behaviors in creative embedded ways on social posts, blogs, at events, and in other tactics.

Stimulus–Response Theory

While social learning theory places emphasis on human proactivity in how they learn, *stimulus–response theory* takes a more reactive view. In the theory, environmental stimuli incite an individual's cognitive and affective (emotional) processes that constitute an "organism" (Mehrabian and Russell 1974). The psychological state of a person (both reason and emotion) acts as an intermediary between the environmental stimuli and a resulting behavior.

The theory acknowledges that there is often a significant environmental "load" of multiple stimuli and that a person's memory is also a factor in responding to and processing multiple stimuli. Emotional responses can include pleasure, arousal, domination, fear, and others. Behavioral responses can be either to approach or avoid a stimulus.

Public relations professionals can learn from this theory that they do not communicate in a vacuum. Public relations messages, from a campaign or routine interactions, are part of this environmental "load" of stimuli. Individuals remember past messages and interactions. Individuals have both emotional and rational responses. Crafting messages to break through the multiple stimuli and to appeal to the appropriate psychological state of recipients is the strategy that will be more effective. Another strategy would be to remind individuals of past messages or interactions to earn attention and a particular response.

Spiral of Silence

The *spiral of silence* is a theory related to public opinion and describes what is often a negative phenomenon. In today's culture, terms related to this theory are "cancel culture" or "self-censorship" (Hobbs and O'Keefe 2024).

Similar to groupthink, but on a larger, societal scale, the spiral of silence describes the phenomenon in which an individual's willingness to express an opinion is dependent on their perception of the public opinion on that topic. If they believe their opinion is consistent with that of the majority, they are more likely to express it. If they believe their opinion is different than that of the majority, they may refrain from expressing it.

"The tendency of the one to speak up and the other to be silent starts off a spiraling process which increasingly establishes one opinion as the prevailing one" (Noelle-Neumann 1974, 44). Restraint from expression could be due to a hostile opinion climate or a fear of a threat of isolation.

Silence may not always be out of fear but could also be polite filtering in the case of a topic that is controversial or that has an element of morality. At the same time, a fear of isolation could encourage opinion expression in a false compliance with popular opinion or what has been called "virtue signaling" (Scheufele and May 2000). Others have found that those willing to self-censor are less likely to express true opinions in either hostile or friendly environments. Opinion expression may also be affected by whether the issue is emerging, enduring, or transitory, with true opinions most likely to be expressed on enduring issues (Gearhardt and Zhang 2018).

Silence can take different forms as different avoidance strategies are used. These include reflecting the question, expressing uncertainty, feigning indifference, discussing another's opinion, changing the topic, pretending to agree vaguely, or outright silence (Hayes 2007).

The news media can also play a part in the spiral of silence when they publicize which opinions are prevalent and which are not, giving validity to one's perception of the popular and acceptable opinion to express. The spiral works as media publicizes a predominant opinion; then individuals either express their opinions or not, based on what is in the news; the media in turn attend to those opinions expressed to report as public opinion; and the expression or silence in response to this media reporting continues (Littlejohn 1989; Noelle-Neumann 1984).

Social media has been shown to accelerate the spiral of silence. In an atmosphere of uncertainty and misinformation, in particular, people are wary of being judged. This leads to them remaining silent. However, when people see their own opinion gaining momentum on social platforms, they are more likely to express their own directly or by sharing others' with whom they agree (Dam et al. 2021).

The lesson for public relations professionals would be caution. When doing research on public opinion, it would be wise to ask questions in an environment that respondents feel is safe to share their true opinion regardless of perceptions of majority views. This may require anonymity or one-on-one interviews without the influence of others. Also, professionals should be cautious about conclusions based on public expression. True majority opinion may not be what some perceive it to be because alternative opinions have not been expressed.

Selective Exposure/Media Use Model

Selective exposure is an old concept that essentially says people pay attention to the media that confirms what they think, their values, or carries the content they seek or are interested in. It means that it cannot be assumed that all media reach all people.

The *media use model* unifies this and several other theories and concepts to expand on media processes and effects (Hoewe and

Ewoldson 2024). Other theories aggregated in this theory include some discussed previously in this book and some coming up in later chapters, including uses and gratifications, elaboration likelihood model, cultivation theory, and more.

The media use model has six propositions or stages during which a person considers existing processing constraints during their selection and interpretation of media content:

1. Expectations, motivations, and individual differences predict an individual's media selection. These variances could be a preference for entertainment versus news content or objectivity versus a perspective.
2. Individuals form impressions of media content as they consume it where coherence with expectations and motivations leads to satisfaction, and incoherence leads to dissatisfaction with the media selected.
3. Coherence will prompt continued consumption of that media content.
4. Incoherence that cannot be resolved will lead to incommensurability, which will prompt the individual to stop consuming that media content.
5. Continued media consumption facilitates subsequent impression formation (i.e., a return to step 2).
6. After stopping consumption of specific media content, the consumer goes back to the media selection process.

This theory, recently proposed, has many applications in an era where "media" includes podcasts, blogs, influencer social channels, as well as the brand journalism publications and other media distributed by organizations directly. Also, many media platforms have a particular ideological perspective that might be an aspect of whether it is coherent and commensurate with a public. Public relations professionals can learn what their target publics' expectations and motivations are to consume information and then seek to consistently satisfy these expectations with the form of content produced.

Digital Media Theories

Theory responds and evolves with changes in culture and technology. As such, a set of theories related specifically to digital media is especially useful. As in other categories of theory, there are theories from other disciplines that inform social media and digital media, in general. Some have called for a unique social media theory specific to public relations (Kent and Li 2020). Part VI of this book covers a variety of theories that are specific to public relations. For now, it is good to preface a list of more general digital media theories with a mix of normative and scientific principles that have been offered in an effort to start building a PR theory of social media:

1. Social media should serve the interests of all publics/stakeholders and not just organizational interests;
2. Genuine social media communications should be based on dialogic engagement rather than faux engagement or message reception;
3. Social media communities are comprised of self-selected networks;
4. Social media spaces are places of culture as much as community;
5. The architecture of social media is not the same as other media;
6. Social media can be a relationship-building tool rather than a marketplace (Kent and Li 2020).

These principles are not codified into theory as yet but serve as a good introduction with a public relations perspective to consider the theories that follow. Consistent themes are that digital media enable and people expect relational communities. Therefore, professionals should see themselves as participants in a conversation more than speakers on a stage.

CHAPTER 8

New Media Theory

New media theory is a body of older theories applied to new, digital contexts (Littlejohn and Foss 2009). Its basic premise is that the Internet is about convergence of media forms, not replacement of one by the other. However, there are differences in new media in terms of how information is shared and how people engage with it. For one, there is more active participation as opposed to passive reception. Face-to-face communication is replaced with ritual and varied forms of intimacy. Identities are different online as opposed to in real life. Digital media is also a stage on which to appear, with democratization of access and the phenomenon of user-generated content.

Generally speaking, for a public relations professional to understand new media, they must understand the complexities of markets, individuals, and technologies. A paradigm shift is expected, and professionals need to let go of the habit to control interactions and understand why audiences are even on a digital medium and then adapt their own perspective about communication and resulting communication behavior. This caution is consistent with some theoretical views about technology and progress. Thomas Kuhn challenged the idea that all accumulation of facts and theories is progress. Instead, he advocated for an episodic view of advancement, in which anomalies interrupt routine scientific work at a slower pace and give rise to a paradigm shift and rapid change (Kuhn 1968). Meanwhile, the notion of the seduction of technology warns that while new technology has an appeal and seems to offer easy solutions, it can also hide negative effects (Alfano et al. 2018).

Computer-Mediated Communication Theory

Computer-mediated communication theory (CMC) emerged as the Internet became ubiquitous. The change that necessitated a new theory is the fact that individuals communicated via the mediation of a computer. It was not face-to-face communication, nor was it mass communication. The theory predicts how individuals form rich, meaningful relationships via CMC (Walther 1992). The theory noted that time was vital to this process as people adapted verbal communications to this online environment—they altered word choice for emphasis and clarity, and they used emoticons as a CMC version of nonverbal cues and symbols. Visual online media, then, can be equal to in-person face-to-face communications.

Later, this theory was extended to describe a range of relational presentations in CMC. On the one extreme, there is the impersonal, where people communicate but do not share personally or form deep relationships. This is followed by a middle range, the interpersonal, which more closely approximates face-to-face communication in person. A new category is the hyperpersonal, where the advances in platforms such as YouTube or Zoom facilitated interpersonal interactions that exceeded intimacy desired or experienced offline (Walther 1996).

More recently, it has been proposed that CMC affects group more than interpersonal communication. When characteristics of a person cannot be seen by individual cues, a person experiences "deindividuation" (Walther 2018). As a result, people relate to each other on the basis of social categories and experience people as ingroup or outgroup. "It is not interpersonal, but inter-group behavior that CMC promotes" (Walther 2018, 89). The "echo chambers" people describe online are less about content than whom people label as friends. Now, "CMC research is more nuanced. Instead of asking are impressions and relationships in CMC intergroup or interpersonal they are asking when are they intergroup and when are they interpersonal" (Walther 2018, 94).

There is probably not a public relations professional who has not watched a YouTube video or attended a Zoom meeting. In fact, there are few who have not created the video or hosted the meeting. But doing so strategically would mean applying some of the theoretical concepts and observations about CMC. First, professionals should consider whether the CMC is merely for convenience or whether it also has equal or superior aspects to in-person communication that will help meet objectives. Also, ask whether the interaction is intended to be interpersonal or group oriented. Then, make a wise choice about how the users will experience the interaction in terms of whether it is impersonal, inter-personal, or hyperpersonal. One factor would be whether the goal is to share information (i.e., more one-way), or solicit input in a two-way interaction. CMC can do both, but it depends on the content, the plat-form, and how the host of the interaction frames the communication interaction.

Dialogic Communication Theory

Dialogue is an older concept, but it has been made new with the emer-gence of digital communication. This is because digital media enables dialogue, but many professionals do not take advantage of that potential. This section brings together a variety of theoretical concepts related to dialogue and their application in digital media under the umbrella of *dialogic communication theory*.

Dialogic communication has been defined as "any negotiated exchange of opinions or ideas" or "interactions between organizations and publics that seek to create mutual respect, mutual understanding and mutual benefits" (Wirtz and Zimbras 2018, 26). Dialogic is not the same as two-way symmetrical communication because it implies equality of power, not just exchange (Wirtz and Zimbras 2018). Two-way symmet-rical communication, as will be explained further in Part VI on theories specific to public relations, implies two-way interactions, in which pro-fessionals may listen and adapt to publics and not merely send one-way messages. However, it does share many specific characteristics of dialogic communication.

Dialogic communication is also considered to be ethically superior to other forms of communication (more on this in Part V) because it es-sentially and theoretically means an orientation to others and recognition of their innate value (Buber 1958; Pearson 1989). True dialogue is said to go beyond superficial; it is more than an organization communicating with stakeholders and getting a response (Lane and Lane 2020). In true dialogue, both parties desire open and respectful interaction (Theunissen and Norbani 2011).

Dialogue also has a variety of unique features as a form of com-munication. These features include *mutuality* (inclusion, collaborative orientation, shared equality); *propinquity* (closeness, immediacy, publics are consulted on matters that affect them, and they feel free to articulate demands to an organization); *empathy* (support, trust, confirmation); *risk* (both parties are vulnerable and take risks in communicating and sharing information); *commitment* to conversation, interpretation being genuine and authentic (Kent and Taylor 2002). Because of these characteristics, "dialogue shifts the focus (of public relations) somewhat by suggesting that our relationships should be centered on long-term, productive engagement with all relevant stakeholders and publics" (Kent and Taylor 2002, 86).

There are a variety of theoretical types of dialogue. These could be viewed by professionals as different purposes for engaging in dialogue with specific publics: to network, to exchange information, to set an agenda, to deliberate, to co-create meaning and value, or to make decisions (Chen et al. 2020). A related typology of forms or purposes of dialogue is presented as a ladder of citizen participation, with the highest rung representing the ideal and the lowest, ethically suspect. From the bottom to the top of the ladder, these forms of dialogue are manipulation, therapy, informing, consultation, placation, partnership, delegated power, and citizen control (Arnstein 1969).

In public relations, the most used concept of dialogic communication is a set of five principles of dialogue. Originally conceived of for websites, they can be considered best practice execution of all digital tactics:

1. Dialogic loop—a feedback loop that allows publics to pose questions and receive answers;
2. Usefulness of information—the information on digital platforms serves the interest of publics and not just the organization;
3. Return visit generation—go beyond content updates to include interactive strategies that intentionally draw people to participate, such as Q&As and time-bound online forums;
4. Interactive interface—logical organization, easy to find information, emphasize content over aesthetic; and
5. Conservation of visitors—limit and use judiciously outbound links, ads, or anything that causes visitors to bounce off a website or keep scrolling in a feed (Kent and Taylor 1998).

A key aspect of dialogue is *engagement*. While mentioned in other theoretical categories, it is especially relevant in digital contexts. It is through engagement that organizations, publics, and stakeholders make decisions that create social capital. According to some scholars, it is both a way for public relations professionals to orient themselves toward digital communication and an approach when executing communications: "We believe the best way to explicate engagement as a foundational public relations concept is to position the discussion of engagement within dialogic theory" (Taylor and Kent 2014, 387).

Taylor and Kent's five proposed components of engagement can be taken as strategic counsel for practice:

1. Only interact after researching issues, publics, culture, and so on.
2. Demonstrate positive regard for stakeholder input, needs.
3. Consider the relational purpose beyond immediate problem or issue.
4. Seek advice and counsel on community, public, organization concern.
5. Contribute to fully functioning society (a normative, ethical term) by recognizing interdependence of organization and publics (Taylor and Kent 2014).

To summarize this lengthy set of theoretical concepts about dialogue and engagement on digital media, recall, as a matter of strategy, that dialogue should serve both public and organizational interest and thus affect social capital. There is a critical need to distinguish genuine dialogue from that which only appears so. Counting likes and comments is not dialogue or engagement. And applying theoretical concepts of dialogue must be genuine: "some practitioners act dialogic online but offline treat publics as a means to an end" (Taylor et al. 2019, 86).

Implementing the set of five principles for website design, mentioned earlier, is an obvious practical application. Another best practice list applies to social media:

1. Talk about what stakeholders want to talk about.
2. Be genuinely social.

3. Create public spaces and nurture collective decision making.
4. Be widely informed and act as an organizational leader and not just a mouthpiece.
5. Maintain a long- versus short-term focus (Taylor et al. 2019).

Digital Rhetorical Theory

Digital rhetorical theory takes ancient concepts of rhetoric (logos, pathos, ethos) and the five canons of rhetoric from Aristotle and Cicero and expands them into a seven-step process to create interactive digital narratives. Steps three and four are additions to the original rhetorical cannon. The process is as follows:

1. Know the audience.
2. Define communication goals.
3. Delivery of message. Consider single or multiple media platforms, and strategically consider how to use features of each platform.
4. Invention. Happens simultaneously with delivery. This includes consideration of the purpose of the narrative and the desired rhetorical message, who the audience is and how they will receive the message and rhetorical style, and which content or means of rhetoric are available in the genre or platform used.
5. Arrangement. Can happen simultaneously and continuously with invention. In classical rhetoric, this would be the order of the speech, but in digital media it is the narrative structure, number of authors and contributors, and so forth.
6. Design. In classic rhetoric this would be grammatical style, but in digital communication it includes factors such as font, color, interactive devices, usability, access, and other aesthetic presentation concerns.
7. Updates. In rhetorical theory, this would be memory and memorability and in digital media should include storage and keeping content current. (Basareba et al. 2021).

All of the steps contribute theoretically and strategically to message effectiveness in a digital environment: "principles of digital rhetoric combined with narrative theory provide a foundation on which to create persuasive nonfiction" (Basareba et al. 2021, 391).

Participatory Culture Theory

One aspect of digital media is that it has democratized the communication process in such a way that all people actively participate in the process. Audiences are no longer passive or even merely interactive: They co-create or independently create content for the online environment. Fans or other groups of people build their own participatory cultures through their own development and interpretation of media content. Various forms of participatory culture, or ways to embrace it, are user-generated content, topic-based online groups within social platforms, unique subeconomies, and transmedia storytelling or "spreadable" media (Jenkins et al. 2013).

The idea behind spreadable media is that it can move across different forms of digital media. Content does not just flow from sender to receiver but circulates top down or bottom up, from grassroots, or from corporate entities. It is also not a one-time distribution. Spreadable media is multimodal and ongoing. The key is that value and meaning are created in multiple "economies," and "if it doesn't spread, it's dead" (Jenkins et al. 2013).

Participatory culture theory calls for a paradigm shift in how professional communicators think about content creation. Companies see content as a commodity that audiences can contribute to and add monetary value. But audiences operate in social reciprocity and see their contributions as adding worth in terms of meaning, if not monetarily, and expect respect and recognition for their participation.

Given this theoretical perspective, public relations professionals should think of digital media not as a new place to target audiences but as a new environment where they must seek permission to participate. The most spreadable and participatory media has intentional gaps in content for publics to insert personal meaning. As such, participatory culture online has the potential to increase diversity and empathy toward multiple communities. Professionals should allow and invite communication contributions from their publics.

Media Richness Theory

Every medium of communication is either "lean" or "rich" based on the ability to carry socio-emotional message content (Carr 2021). Media Richness theory proposes that lean media are good for raw data, whereas rich media are good to provide many social cues and transmit a sense of social presence.

Publics have two types of information needs, according to this theory. One is to reduce uncertainty; this would call for concrete and specific information that enables an individual to decide. Another type of information need is to reduce equivocality or enable an ability to identify one option among several. Equivocality can also be considered ambiguity or lack of clarity on a complex topic (Carr 2021).

Given these theoretical concepts, public relations professionals can strategically select media—lean or rich—appropriate for the information needs of publics on a given topic or message. Even in digital media, there is a place for simple and textual presentation of information, which would be lean and useful to reduce uncertainty. But in other cases where publics want to reduce equivocality and narrow down options, rich media that employs video, interactivity, and other unique digital features would be more strategic as well as sought and appreciated by publics.

Theory of Electronic Propinquity

Propinquity is a word most likely found only in theoretical articles and books. It was mentioned previously in this section on digital communication in association with dialogue. Again, it means "the perception of relational or psychological closeness toward another person" (Carr 2021, 53). It should be obvious to public relations professionals who understand that the basis of the profession is to build relationships that propinquity is a good thing.

The *theory of electronic propinquity* argues that in a digital media environment, there are several factors that affect propinquity in a given channel:

- Bandwidth—the channel's capacity to carry multiple cues (rich);
- Mutual directionality—the channel facilitates quick feedback;

- Task complexity—less complex tasks lead to greater propinquity, but complex interactions lead to a focus on the task more than the relationship;
- Communication skills—greater skills at creating and interpreting cues to meaning lead to greater propinquity;
- Communication rules—more technical and social guidelines constrain interactions and reduce propinquity; and
- Available media choices—more choices equal less propinquity because users do not have to work hard to make the most of a particular channel and construct messages carefully and meaningfully (Karzenny 1978).

Again, public relations professionals who want to build and maintain relationships with publics that are mutually beneficial and have a closeness—propinquity—can establish objectives and develop strategies and tactics with these factors in mind. Other strategic applications include offering unique content relevant to publics, don't limit forms of response, and allow and invite publics to initiate the topics of communication.

Strategic Summary of Part III—Media

It is a significant mistake for a public relations professional to choose a communication tactic without considering whether that tactic or channel is appropriate for the intended public, topic, message, and objective. The variety of media theories in this chapter lead to a variety of useful factors to think about before selecting a tactic.

- Public relations professionals can participate with the news media in setting the agenda for public discussion or contribute to determining what subjects people are talking about.
- There are many factors beyond news judgment that determine when the news media communicate specific news.
- The quality is more important than the quantity of message exposure over time to lead individuals to a certain perspective on a topic.

- The distinction between public and private identities has eroded, making audiences more emotional than rational when interpreting messages.
- How a message is framed in terms of highlighting what is most important and what it means contributes significantly to audience understanding.
- Publics often learn not just from public relations messages but by observing others.
- Publics are overstimulated with messages and respond to emotional lures and reminders of past messages in this environment.
- Individuals are reluctant to express themselves if they perceive their position is not consistent with the majority, and this could lead to public relations professionals misunderstanding true public opinion.
- People evaluate messages and relationships with other people and organizations based on whether their expectations for interactions are met or not.
- Social media is seen by many to be for relationships rather than as a marketplace.
- CMC can be similar to face-to-face or group communication but has unique features that should be employed to be successful.
- Dialogue, particularly online, has a series of features that make it distinct from engagement and two-way communication. Success depends on understanding and employing these features.
- An advanced view of communication considers audiences as participants and co-creators of content that requires professionals to be humble and empathic in interactions.
- The concept of propinquity, or perception of relational and psychological closeness, is an important strategic goal for public relations interactions to be successful.

PART IV

Persuasion Theories—Going Beyond Awareness

There are two statements frequently heard from coworkers or clients in the context of planning a public relations campaign or tactic. They are similar in meaning and can be frustrating to the experienced public relations professional. One is "we just need to get the word out," and the other is "we just need to raise awareness."

The simple adverb "just" is the first offense. It implies that a minimal effort is needed. The phrases "raise awareness" or "get the word out" are also annoying because they diminish the profession of public relations. It perpetuates the myth that public relations is only about pushing information one way. It also implies that doing so yields results, as if raising awareness or getting the word out is the end of the story, mission accomplished, objective achieved.

Of course, as previous chapters should have indicated, making people aware is merely a first step. Objectives for public relations need to go beyond output—what practitioners accomplish in terms of messages and tactics—and should focus on *outcome—a change in the attitudes, opinions, and/or behaviors of designated publics.* That requires far more than getting some nebulous word out or merely making people aware of something.

In theoretical terms, the idea of merely getting attention and assuming changes will occur in people is outdated theory. In the 1920s and 1930s, there was a popular theory, alternatively called *magic bullet theory* or *hypodermic needle theory*, that basically claimed that the media or professional communicators could inject messages into a passive, homogeneous public and they would all respond immediately (Lowery 1995). What is disturbing is that this notion of mass immediate influence of populations was associated with Nazi propaganda techniques (Lasswell 1927).

Since then, theory and practice in public relations has come a long way. While public relations is essentially about relationships, it is in the context of those relationships that persuasion needs to happen. Part IV explains a variety of theories that are useful to strategically—and ethically—persuade individuals and groups of people. The first set of theories will show, contrary to hypodermic needle theory, that strategy is necessary even to get people to pay attention. It is never automatic or assumed. A second set of theories is about understanding and affecting attitudes and opinions, or a cognitive and affective response. The final section of theories is focused on motivating people to change behavior or take an initial action. Awareness, attitude, and action are often considered the three specific categories of output objectives a public relations professional would have in a campaign. The theories will help form strategies specific to achieving each type of objective.

CHAPTER 9

Persuasive Theories Affecting Attention

Anyone who has children or has taught a class, given a speech, or run a meeting knows that getting and keeping attention is not a given. For the public relations professional, a "spray and pray" approach to flooding newsrooms with news releases or a spam-level repetition of e-mail appeals is neither a wise nor an effective means of gaining attention. Strategy is required behind the message content, the channel, and the frequency. This set of theories can help professionals do more than "just" get the word out.

Cognitive Dissonance

Cognitive, relating to cognition, essentially means acquiring knowledge or understanding or, even more basically, thinking. Dissonance is a term from music and describes the opposite of harmony. In other words, something is "out of tune," clashing, or at odds with something else.

So cognitive dissonance is a condition when someone has two opposing or clashing ideas in mind at the same time. The writer F. Scott Fitzgerald, in a 1936 essay in *Esquire Magazine*, penned a line that became famous: "The test of a first-rate intelligence is the ability to hold two opposed ideas in the mind at the same time, and still retain the ability to function." Unfortunately, *cognitive dissonance theory* asserts that even intelligent people seek to maximize internal psychological consistency (Festinger 1957). Put another way, people want to avoid what some psychologists call "cognitive pain" resulting from conflicting ideas or thoughts. Because of this, people try to resolve the "problem" of two opposing ideas in their minds by rejecting one of them. Often, they reject new ideas or messages in order to maintain their current attitude or disposition. The theory points out that people will selectively pay attention to information that confirms their current mindset. They will also quickly reject or not even pay attention to new information seen as contradictory to that mindset. This happens in a neurological nanosecond, so they do not even pay attention to new messages.

The size of the problem, or "magnitude of dissonance," is affected by the complexity of the opposing ideas. The more complex or nuanced each idea is, the greater the cognitive pain. This is why some people try to simplify concepts or just avoid thinking about an issue altogether. At the same time, the dissonance is greater the more the issue has personal relevance or importance to an individual. This means public relations professionals need to think not just about getting attention but about attracting full attention such that people understand before dismissing a message.

Public relations professionals need to consider that their intended audiences may have predispositions or existing attitudes with which their message will conflict. It is important, therefore, not just to simply present a position. Rather, a professional will need to present a position in a less "painful" way in order for readers to give it some consideration. Professionals should encourage people not to merely consider a different idea but to start from square one and reevaluate their opinion, putting two ideas on an even plane; not a current versus old idea but one versus another worth equal consideration. It is also strategically important to keep communicating to audiences who already agree with a position to bolster it and avoid a change of attitude or opinion from contrary messages.

Another strategic consideration is the weak and temporary effect of incentives or attempts to induce compliance, such as coupons or other attractive promises to those who change their mind or behavior. A one-time behavior is not indicative of lasting attitude change.

Yet another facet of cognitive dissonance theory has to do with consistence of thought and behavior. Many people think one way and act another. This applies to everything from health behavior to purchase intention to acting on a promise to support a cause. Exposing this "hypocrisy," a form of cognitive dissonance (thought vs. action) can lead a person to seek consistency by changing either their thought or behavior. Professionals need to be careful to move people in the right direction and not to offend when exposing hypocrisy—persuasion should be encountered as a helpful nudge and not an accusation.

Elaboration Likelihood Model

The degree to which a person is persuaded—or not—by a public relations message is dependent on how hard they are thinking about the topic or how focused they are on the message. Most people think they can multitask but have to acknowledge the difference between skimming something or really reading deeply. This is the essence of the *elaboration likelihood model* (ELM) (Petty and Cacioppo 1981, 1986a, 1986b).

Elaboration in this model means *issue-relevant thinking*, or how hard someone processes information they receive on a given issue. This is not an either/or proposition—elaboration happens on a scale.

ELM describes two "routes" of thinking, or pathways that messages travel in someone's mind. These could also be considered strategically as two pathways to persuasion:

- *The central route*—in this route, people are focused and thinking directly about the topic at hand. In this route, elaboration is high.
- *The peripheral route*—similar to peripheral vision, in which people see things indirectly off to the side, this is the thought pattern in ELM. In this route, people are reading or hearing information, but they are not giving it their full or direct attention (i.e., elaboration is low). This is often because the issue or topic is not perceived as important or personally relevant to them.

Again, the central and peripheral routes are not an either/or phenomenon, but they exist as extremes at the ends of a scale. An individual is more or less one way or the other, and it changes over time and by topic. What is helpful to public relations professionals is this: The emphasis in messaging will be more effective if it considers whether the reader will process it more centrally or peripherally.

- If a reader is using the central route and elaboration is high, then the *message content* itself is the most persuasive. This means the argument must be strong, well reasoned, and clearly and compellingly written;
- If a reader is using the peripheral route and elaboration is low, then *cognitive shortcuts and peripheral cues* are most persuasive.

Research has found seven peripheral cues that could be considered as strategies for professionals communicating to a public likely to have low involvement for a topic. Persuasive messages could include one or several of these cues as message appeals:

1. Authority—the perception that someone is an authority on the topic;
2. Commitment—the perception that the communicator is committed to the topic, issue, cause, or audience;
3. Contrast—the message theme is better than another by comparison;
4. Liking—an affinity toward a person, place, or organization;
5. Reciprocity—the message seems to offer a deal or presents what an audience will gain from attending to the message or changing attitude;
6. Scarcity—the individual is concerned about missing an opportunity, even if it is a false urgency; and
7. Social proof—peer pressure, or the message is from a similar individual or mentions people in the recipient's peer group who have already adopted an attitude or behavior (Cialdini 1993).

Uses and Gratifications Theory

A vital principle in gaining attention is acknowledging that paying attention is the choice of the audience, not something that a professional can direct. Another way of saying this is that media use and attention is not passive or coerced and that the power is in the audience not the media or communicator (Katz et al. 1973, 1974).

The idea that people use media to gratify a personal need, and hence *uses and gratifications theory*, came to be when radio was the exciting new media. A study of women who listened to daytime radio serials determined that it filled a need for them and that needs varied by individuals, contradicting again hypodermic needle theory (Herzog 1944).

Years of study since the 1940s developed the theory into three assumptions: Audiences are active and goal-directed, they are responsible for choosing media to meet needs, and the news media compete with other sources of information to gratify people's needs (Palmgreen 1984). The competition with the media to gratify audience needs reassures public relations professionals that tactics other than earned media have long been necessary and effective. Factors in audiences determining sources for need fulfillment range from social, psychological, and cultural to values-based (Palmgreen 1984).

Other scholars have extended the theory to develop typologies of people's needs that could be fulfilled by media, either news media or public relations tactics. One typology of needs focused on television included a diversion from reality, to develop personal relationships, affirm personal identity, or surveillance and observation of society and culture (McQuail et al. 1972). A broader view of mass communication developed another list of needs people seek to satisfy with media consumption: Get advice on everyday life, obtain tools for social advance, prepare mentally to engage others, provide a basis to plan for the day, or to acquire reassurance (Katz et al. 1974).

The application of uses and gratifications theory for public relations professionals requires some simple humility. It is not all about the organization's needs. The appeal should not be what the organization needs from the public but how the organization and its information can meet a need of a specific audience. Too much public relations effort seems to be yelling "Pay attention to us!" even as the audience replies, "What's in it for me?" The public relations professional who makes the answer to that question obvious will have people's attention.

CHAPTER 10

Theories Affecting Attitude and Opinion

If making people aware can be accomplished by reaching them with a message and getting them to pay attention, getting them to change their mind is a greater challenge. This is the flaw in much public relations practice—assuming that influencing what people think about automatically influences what they think. But people can remain indifferent, hold on to existing opinions, or adopt a competing point of view based on competing messages and other social and psychological factors (Cialdini 1994). This group of theories explains those factors that affect how people think about and respond to messages. Such knowledge is a vital asset in strategic public relations efforts to persuade.

Attribution Theory

A key factor in people forming opinions and attitudes is their perception of the causes of others' statements and behaviors. People attribute a cause or assume an intention behind someone's message or actions, and this attribution is a key factor in their resulting opinion or attitude about the message or the source of the message.

Attribution theory was first applied to individuals and personal achievement (Weiner 1972, 1995). However, the theory has been shown to apply to corporate actors as well and was the foundation for situational crisis communication theory (SCCT) to be discussed in Part VI. Research has shown that people weigh whether a cause is primarily internal or external. They are more likely to punish an actor or have a negative attitude if they think the actor was the cause of a negative situation (high internal attribution) and if they think other factors did not contribute to the situation (low external attribution). The converse is also true in cases where a person attributes something not so much to the actor as to external factors. In such cases, their attitude toward the actor will be positive (Jeong 2009).

Time and complexity are also factors in opinions. If the public sees an actor and cause co-vary (associated with each other) over time, the attribution of the actor as cause is stronger. This, of course, relates to reputation. Meanwhile, if the public perceives several potential causes of a situation, the attribution of the actor as the cause is discounted.

There is a three-stage process to attributing a statement or action to a person or organization: First, the behavior is observed and perceived; second, the behavior is determined to be intentional; and third, the behavior is attributed to internal or external causes. The perception and attribution are based on several dimensions: the internal or external control; the stability of causes over time; and whether the actor was in control of the cause or not (Jeong 2009).

A practical way of thinking of attribution theory is that publics do not only consider the content of what a message says but weigh why they think a person or organization is saying it. Statements like "they are only saying that because…." or "they are doing that now because …" are attribution theory in action. Public relations professionals can ensure positive attitudes by addressing the potential of negative attributions that might lead to negative attitudes and opinions. When making a statement or announcing an activity, the mere facts are not enough. Offering the rationale with transparency can make the difference between acceptance or rejection, between a positive or negative attitude among publics. In fact, one study employed a measurement instrument and determined that organizations are more likely to be trusted when they allow and encourage public participation, share substantial information, give balanced reports, and are open to public scrutiny and accountability (Rawlins 2008). Communicating and demonstrating honest and legitimate intent behind statements and actions, and being consistent over time, will engender a positive reputational attitude that will contribute to positive attitudes and message reception in the future.

Co-orientation Theory

Another theory based on the concept of perceptions affecting meaning is *co-orientation theory*. The premise of the theory is that "a person's behavior is not only based on his private cognitive construction of his world; it is also a function of his perception of the orientations held by others around him and of his orientation to them" (McLeod and Chaffee 1973, 470). The orientations can be in interpersonal, small group, or large societal settings. The perceptions a person has toward others affects their own attitudes and behaviors.

The roots of the theory are in the concept that two people can be attracted to each other positively or negatively and are simultaneously co-oriented to an object of communication, such as a topic, issue, or cause (Newcomb 1953). If there are different evaluations (opinions) of that object, there is tension in the relationship. The tension can be resolved in numerous ways: by changing the attitude toward the other or the topic; by trying to persuade the other to adapt one's own opinion; to stop communicating with the other; to seek support from an additional other who shares the opinion; or to cognitively distort perception of reality of the tense situation.

The application of co-orientation theory has a lot to do with the notion of managing expectations, because in many professional relationships, expectations can be implicit or explicit and variance in expectations is the cause of relational tension (Rogers and Andrews 2013). A public relations professional could have a competitive advantage if they manage expectations and lead to a sustained and positive co-orientation of opinions in various relationships. This could be true in numerous contexts of public relations practice, such as an agency and client in a request for proposals (RFP) situation, a public relations department presenting its plan to management, or the organization and its publics in the execution of a campaign. In all cases, the communicator's style and content should adapt to the recipient's attitudes and perspectives and not assume agreement or neutrality. Some conversation with or research on the recipient's orientation prior to communicating enables a professional to strategically appeal to the correct mindset with realistic goals. Building relationships and seeking mutual understanding if not outright persuasion may be better than blunt attempts at changing others. It is strategic to think long term.

Inoculation Theory

Hypodermic needle theory was discussed earlier as a dated and ineffective theory. *Inoculation theory* also employs a medical metaphor, but it is more current and practically useful.

An inoculation in a medical sense is to give a person a small dose of a virus in order to build up natural antibodies, and thus can a person protect themself against a potential attack of the actual virus.

As a communication theory, then, the idea is to give people just a little of an opposite view and give them defenses against it for future thought (McGuire 1964). The two components are a threat, or a forewarning, that someone may hear this attack on their current beliefs, and then a preemptive refutation in which arguments against the opposite opinion are raised. In one study, subjects who were inoculated with messages that were supportive of a desired opinion, refutational of potential attack messages, or a combination resisted persuasion by passively receiving attack messages or actively encoding them. There was variance by the type of attack message and the intensity of language (Burgoon and King 1974).

The practical value of inoculation theory is the means to maintain positive opinions. It is foolish to achieve an attitude or opinion change and assume it will be stable in a dynamic and complex world of changing situations and competing messages. The "goal is to persuade someone not to be persuaded" by helping them develop resistance to counterarguments (Dainton and Zelley 2023, 27). The theory "offers an innovative powerful way to guide public relations campaigns, with established efficacy in crisis and risk communications" (Compton et al. 2021).

One aspect of inoculation theory is self-disclosure, in which an organization shares negative information about itself to mitigate negative attitude and opinion formation before third parties can expose the organization (Compton et al. 2021; Easley et al. 1995). This strategic application of the theory could provide protection against negative messages from news coverage, consumer groups, or competitors. It is the theoretical basis of the common crisis strategy of "getting in front of the issue" or "controlling the narrative." A self-disclosure strategy is most effective when specific negative information is known or could become public, a refutation of specific negative claims is possible, and the threat of damage to current opinions of key publics is high.

There are other specific public relations practice areas beyond crisis communication where inoculation theory has been studied and found useful. The theory has been applied as a model for public relations campaigns (Crowley and Hoyer 1994), in corporate advertising

(Kim 2013; Ho et al. 2016), in investor relations to encourage investors to stay in the market (Dillingham and Ivanov 2017), to combat customer dissatisfaction (Mikolen et al. 2015), and to protect against negative attacks on social media (Haigh and Wigley 2015).

Inoculation theory is obviously relevant as a messaging strategy, but it also relates to the larger emphasis in public relations on building and maintaining relationships. Some scholars advise that public relations professionals use inoculation theory as a type of dialogue, in which publics are allowed to make their own decisions and enhance their critical thinking and the organization participates with its public to determine meaning (Compton et al. 2021).

Social Judgment Theory

The essence of *social judgment theory* is that messages produce change through judgmental processes and effects (Brehmer 1988). In other words, the persuasiveness of writing depends a lot on the way the recipient evaluates it. And what readers evaluate is not the quality or style or creativity of writing—they evaluate the position taken in messages and how that position is presented.

A key concept in this theory is "latitudes." A globe or map has lines of longitude (the north–south lines) and latitude (east–west). Taken together, longitude and latitude help determine a position on the globe. That global position makes more sense when considered relative to other positions on the globe.

In social judgment theory, it is a given that there are several potential "positions" on any given topic or issue. Just as in the geographic example cited previously, people's attitudes about a position that an organization may be advocating is evaluated relative to other positions about which they are aware. Given this, people do not simply agree or disagree with the position that someone is trying to persuade them to adopt. Rather, their assessment of a position falls into a range, or latitude of "acceptance," "noncommittal," or "rejection" relative to someone else's current reference point or anchor based on their own experience, where anchoring can be seen as how strongly the individual, group or organization is committed to the attitude object. The key is that there are a range of positions and a degree of agreement (acceptance, noncommittal, or rejection) with each one (Sherif and Hovland 1961).

Another concept in social judgment theory is ego-involvement, which means a person's stand on an issue is central to their sense of self (i.e., ego). If a person has a direct personal connection to an issue or topic or they believe they have been strongly affected by that topic either negatively or positively, they will have more than a casual interest in the subject. They will be high in ego-involvement (Sherif and Hovland 1961). Obviously, an ego-involved audience will be more firmly anchored in their position regarding the attitude object.

This is important because as the degree of ego-involvement increases, the size of the latitude of rejection also increases. So more positions proposed to such a person will fall into the latitude of rejection, and only proposals in their narrow latitude of acceptance will be able to persuade them. Put bluntly, it is much more difficult to change the minds or rally support for people with a high ego-involvement because they evaluate messages not just on arguments alone but how closely those arguments appeal to their experience, identity, or sense of self.

Because people evaluate positions relative to others or their own, social judgment theory also points out the phenomena or effects of assimilation and contrast. An assimilation effect occurs when a person perceives a message to be advocating a position closer to their own than it actually is. A contrast effect describes a situation where a person perceives a message to be advocating a position farther from their own than it actually is.

Note that it all depends on a person's perception. A message perceived in the latitude of acceptance is more likely to be assimilated as the same as their own view even if there is a slight difference. A message perceived in the latitude of rejection is more likely to be contrasted with their own view even more than it is. It is as if they say "close enough" or that an argument is "just too extreme." If a message lands in someone's latitude of acceptance, there is greater likelihood of attitude change. If there is a large discrepancy between current attitude and the message, but the message is still in the latitude of acceptance, there will be even more attitude change. If a message falls in a latitude of rejection, there will be no attitude change, and, in fact, their current attitude may be reinforced or the message may boomerang against the messenger.

Unfortunately, many unethical writers may use this knowledge to exploit perception to win over people to a specific position. This is why some communicators employ "purposeful ambiguity." Or, writers can unintentionally cause readers to "overreact" to a message by not writing carefully.

However, social judgment theory can be applied ethically and strategically. To avoid the effect of inaccurate assimilation or contrast, clarity of writing and transparency of intent are key to avoid chances of misperception. To be more effective in changing or reinforcing opinions, a professional must know, acknowledge, or appeal to a public's current experience and opinions. Understanding that opinions are not either/or but on a scale opens many avenues for effective persuasion. Acknowledging that a proposed position is not exactly like that of the recipient's but better than alternatives in a latitude of rejection could lead to agreement or acceptance of an organization's point of view.

What makes social judgment theory attractive to strategic public relations is that once a professional has identified where on the continuum of acceptance to rejection of the attitude object and the assessed ego-involvement of the audience is, it is possible to create multiple messages aimed close to the level of acceptance that should produce an assimilation effect. Preparing your message strategy as multiple messages, each moving closer to the anchored audience position, will provide a systematic and comprehensive messaging plan. As noted, a single message does not change audience attitude, but multiple messages moving the audience to accept your position may produce the desired attitude change and, ultimately, behavior.

CHAPTER 11

Theories Affecting Motivation and Action

Getting attention is fundamental. Changing attitudes and opinions is more of a challenge. The most difficult task for a public relations professional is to motivate publics to change what they do. Often, changing a behavior or taking initial action is dependent on, first, developing a positive attitude, as discussed in the previous section. The theories in this section uncover the cognitive and social factors that influence people to act.

Theory of Planned Behavior

Sometimes, before a person takes an action, they have to develop an intention to act. In other words, people don't usually act immediately or reactively but begin to think positively about an action and make a plan to act. This can be considered a step between attitude and action and is the basis of the theory of planned behavior.

But human behavior is not always determined by willingness. In other words, some people may agree that taking a particular action is a good idea, but other factors such as time, money, and having adequate information or personal ability may be barriers to action. The theory of planned behavior asserts that actual behavior of individuals is determined by attitude, subjective norms, and their perceived behavioral control (Azjen 1991). A subjective norm is "the likelihood that important referent individuals or groups approve or disapprove of performing a given behavior" (Azjen 1991, 195). It can be considered a form of peer pressure or affirmation. Personal behavioral control varies by context and the particular behavior. It is not exactly the same as actual control but relates to perceptions of one's ability or self-efficacy to successfully and independently perform a behavior: It "refers to the perceived ease or difficulty of performing the behavior and it is assumed to reflect past experiences as well as anticipated impediments or obstacles" (Azjen 1991, 188).

Behavioral intention is high when the attitude toward the behavior is positive, the subjective norm is high, and the perceived behavioral control is strong. Therefore, public relations messages should not merely command or suggest someone enact a behavior. Messages need to address the idea from this theory that people need to be prodded to develop a behavioral intention and overcome perceived obstacles to acting. So, to put it simply, messages should not just say "do this" but rather "you will benefit by doing this" (positive attitude toward behavior), "you should do this because others like you are doing this" (subjective norm), or "you can do this" (perceived behavioral control).

Diffusion of Innovation

It is often the case that when public relations professionals are trying to encourage a change in behavior, it is associated with communicating about a new idea, program, or product. When something is new, it is adopted by the public at a varied rate, for different reasons, by a process. Several theories address this, one of them being diffusion of innovation theory, which is essentially an explanation of how new things spread (Rogers 1962).

The innovation can be either a literally new product or service or even a significant enhancement or differentiation of something current. The key is the perception of newness by the public (Rogers 1962). Innovations that are likely to spread through the public and be adapted as such have five characteristics: a relative advantage to whatever is current; compatibility with lifestyles and current practices; a level of complexity that does not deter adaptation; trialability, or the ability to test before adapting; and observability, or seeing others who may be influential adapting the innovation (Rogers 1962).

There are also five stages in a process of adapting an innovation. Public relations professionals should communicate appropriate messages for each stage of the process to strategically and patiently move publics to adapt whatever it is that is new. The stages with associated public relations objectives are the following:

1. Knowledge (exposure to the innovation);
2. Persuasion (favorable attitude to the innovation);
3. Decisions (encourage choice to adopt innovation);
4. Implementation (invite use or trial);
5. Confirmation (reinforce and encourage continuation of adoption of innovation) (Carden 2008).

People adapt at a different pace, and public relations professionals need to communicate to each group differently according to where they are on a bell curve of adaptation rate. About 2.5 percent of the public are innovators and risk takers and the first to adapt. These are followed by early adopters (about 13.5 percent of the public) who are often respected opinion leaders and vary based on the nature of the innovation. A larger group, 34 percent, are considered an early majority who tend to deliberate longer and follow the lead of early adopters. Once this group adopts an innovation, it is a tipping point of 50 percent. The next group, another 34 percent, are late adopters who tend toward being skeptical and cautious. A final group is the 16 percent of laggards or the long tail of an adoption curve who are suspicious of innovations and resistant to change until that change seems ubiquitous. Public relations professionals can communicate to these groups differently based on their psychological attitude toward innovations and the rate at which they change their behavior accordingly. Using one group as influencers and testimonials to move the other groups is a common strategy (Carden 2008).

Trans-Theoretical Model

There are several other theories or models of persuasive communication that posit that people go through a series of stages as they are persuaded to take action or change their behavior.

The trans-theoretical model (TTM) combines a number of these other models and theories and proposes that people go through a related but different set of five stages compared with the stages in the first two theories in this section. TTM is often associated with health communication but can be broadly applied (Prochaska et al. 1998).

The stages of an individual's thought processes and behavior are precontemplation, contemplation, planning, action, and maintenance. Public relations professionals should develop communication strategies for each stage in a long-term, multiphase campaign. Some of these strategies could be employed in a single message, or they may be communicated in a series of messages over time.

In the precontemplation stage, a person is not yet considering the change in behavior. To hit them at this point with heavy persuasion would be counterproductive. It is best to gently introduce them to the idea or issue and related behavior and focus on awareness about the possibility of an idea or action.

In the contemplation stage, a person is thinking about the possibility of change and needs to be made to think positively about it and be encouraged in their ability to adopt the idea or behavior. The objective at this stage is attitude formation without an explicit call to action just yet.

In the planning stage, people have made a decision to change or act and need to be persuaded to actually go through with it. A message with a clear call to action focused on encouragement and motivation acknowledging and appealing to a decision already made will be most effective.

The action stage is when a person actually enacts a behavior or adopts an attitude. Persuasive messages should be celebratory and encouraging to reinforce the change.

The maintenance stage is after an individual has made a change and must be encouraged to maintain a point of view or continue a behavior. It is always possible, especially in a context where there are competing messages and influences, that a person be persuaded to return to prior opinion or let behavior lapse or return to contradictory behavior.

Reasoned Action Theory

Reasoned action theory is another theory that explains behavior being the result of a person's careful thinking and intentions about the behavior (Fishbein and Ajzen 1975). Some concepts from previous theories are reflected here. According to reasoned action theory, a person's intent to take an action is based on four things:

- *A person's attitude toward the behavior.* If they consider doing something, are they thinking positively or negatively about it? Buying a car, quitting smoking, attending an event, registering for a seminar—all of these are things a person may be positively or negatively inclined toward. Obviously, a positive attitude would more likely lead to actually doing the considered behavior and may only need a nudge, while a negative attitude would require more persuasion.
- *Injunctive norm.* This theoretical term quite simply means that a person is persuaded in part by whether they think that people important to them want them to do a certain behavior. For example, "my spouse wants me to buy this car," "my friends want me to quit smoking," "my coworkers want me to attend this event," and so on are persuasive ingredients to someone's consideration.
- *Descriptive norm.* Unlike considering whether other people want them to do something, the descriptive norm involves someone thinking about whether others do the behavior themselves. For example, others have bought the same car, others have quit smoking, others have registered for an event. It is a form of "peer pressure," but it also just shows the behavior being considered is "normative," not something uniquely unusual, and therefore easier for a person to do.
- *Perceived behavioral control.* According to reasoned action theory, a key factor in considering whether to do a behavior or not is a person's own feeling of "self-efficacy" or their ability to complete the task or successfully do the behavior under consideration. If they don't feel capable or perceive the behavior as too difficult to accomplish, it will be harder to persuade them to do it.

Persuasion can be complicated according to this theory because all four of these factors may apply but are weighted differently (i.e., more or less important) on any given issue. The strategy would then be to appeal to the factor that is likely most important on any issue or weave several or all into a persuasive message. Of course, some research prior to communicating can add confidence about which factor should be the primary focus of an appeal strategy. There are some specific strategic ideas to consider based on this theory.

A professional can influence the attitude toward the behavior by encouraging a reader to reevaluate their existing beliefs about it, diminish the strength of a negative attitude, and stress other beliefs about the behavior.

A strategy may be to respond to the injunctive norm by referring to it if the influential "others" are encouraging the desired behavior or bolster an individual's independence to disregard that other if they are discouraging a behavior.

With regard to the descriptive norm, a public relations professional can make obvious the fact that others are doing the desired behavior (either using a single anecdote example or statistically showing a large number) or that others are not doing a behavior the professional wishes a reader to stop, such as in a cessation campaign in health care.

To encourage a reader's sense of self-efficacy or potential to complete a behavior, it would be good strategy to remove (or verbally diminish) actual or perceived obstacles to doing the behavior, create an opportunity to successfully do behavior (physically or induce mental rehearsal), provide examples of role models or "persons like them" doing the behavior, or offer simple encouragement.

Strategic Summary of Part IV—Persuasion

If getting attention can be a challenge, causing key publics to change their attitudes and behaviors is even more difficult. But once again, insights from persuasion theories give public relations practitioners strategies and a level of confidence that they can achieve outcome objectives in various types of campaigns.

- Getting people to compare the merits of two opposing ideas is more persuasive than using an incentive in an appeal.

- People really focused on an issue are more persuaded by the message, whereas people thinking only indirectly about an issue are more likely to be persuaded by emotion and nonverbal or peripheral cues.
- Understanding the reason people use a medium and appealing to that will help messages penetrate and persuade.
- People don't just pay attention to words but often consider what they perceive to be the reason an organization is saying or doing something when responding to a message.
- Professionals can be more persuasive if they manage their publics' expectations about their mutual interest, concern, opinion, and other orientations with an organization.
- Sharing a little of an opposing opinion and then refuting it can be effective in persuading publics to adopt an organization's point of view or encouraging publics not to be persuaded toward alternative views.
- Professionals do not always need to convince publics to adopt a specific opinion but can present their opinion as one in a range of potential points of view that would be acceptable if not identical to the public's current position.
- People make changes in a planned series of cognitive phases. A series of messages over time that move people gradually to each mindset is more effective at persuasion than one bold appeal at causing immediate change.
- People adopt new ideas at different rates by comparing what is new with what is present, observing others adopt what is new, and trying the change themselves. Communicating in ways that foster each step is more effective than announcing something is new and hoping the novelty alone persuades.
- Professionals should not assume publics are aware of something when they move to change attitudes and behaviors. Sending messages that address people in a latent or precontemplative stage before more direct persuasion will yield higher numbers of those who change attitudes or behaviors.

- People often think of others when considering changing their perspective or behavior. They attend to what they think those they respect would want them to do, and they are moved when others they observe have made the change.
- Professionals should directly address potential resistance to change, such as a person's belief they are not capable of changing, in order to persuade effectively.

PART V

Ethical Theories— Doing It Right and Doing the Right Thing

Part IV on persuasion revealed useful theories and concepts for public relations professionals to persuade publics. It was noted that persuasion can be done unethically, which would be manipulation or deception, or it can be done ethically, which is often called advocacy of a point of view in a transparent manner. Knowing the difference and how to practice ethically is vital for anyone who works in public relations, most of whom strive to be good professionals. In fact, some have said that unethical public relations workers are mere "practitioners" and that only those who practice ethically deserve to be called "professionals." Given the relational nature of public relations, and the management incentive to avoid crises, ethics is eminently tied to strategy as well.

However, ethics is not a simple black and white proposition of doing good and avoiding bad. There is not a categorical measure of ethical or unethical (Bang 2019). The ethical path is not always clear even if a professional seeks to practice ethically. The role of public relations exists between organizations and their many publics, seeking a balance of interests, needs, and perspectives. The resulting ethical dilemmas in which public relations professionals find themselves have been categorized as between an organization and society, between transactional or bonding relationships, and between an individual role as an employee or citizen (Gaara et al. 2024). There are many gray areas in ethics for the myriad of situations in which professionals finds themselves conflicted and have to make quick decisions balancing the desire for a successful campaign with the desire to avoid ethical missteps. Knowledge of ethical theory is useful because it "enables practitioners to assess and respond to ethical situations" (Bang 2019, 67).

Apart from the individual, public relations as an occupation has a general problem that many associate it as an entirely unethical profession, assuming the intent of all public relations is to spin, lie, deceive, or "cast an organization in a positive light" in spite of the reality. However, public relations scholars in the area of ethics have asserted that public relations is an ethical profession: "normatively, public relations management functions with the intent to create understanding rather than deceive" (Bowen 2008, 161). In fact, public relations is well suited to acting as the ethical conscience for an entire organization—not just the public relations department—because of its focus on all publics and mutually beneficial relationships.

Chapters 12 and 13 on ethics theory will help fuse public relations goals with ethical practice. It should help professionals see public relations as inherently ethical, if practiced appropriately, and consistent with theoretical standards for practice. Ethical theories also give confidence that a professional can do the right thing both strategically and ethically. Chapter 12 covers foundational ethical philosophies from the ancients. Chapter 13 brings in ethical theories specifically related to public relations, and Chapter 14 offers practical examples of ethical decision-making models and some perspective on codes of ethics and ethical organizational culture.

CHAPTER 12

Classical Ethical Theories

The subject of ethics has been important since the time of the ancient Greeks. Much of the philosophy of ethics still prominently features Aristotle, Sophocles, and others even as the foundational principles are applied to modern times and specific contexts. Public relations scholars who study and write about ethics also include these classic ethical theories as relevant to public relations (Bang 2019; Bowen 2008; Gower 2003; Davidson 2020). A variety of common classical ethical philosophies that have been associated with and applied to public relations are listed here. Many entire books were written about each theory, and they are significantly summarized here. Note that none are simple, perfect, or universally applicable, and some even contradict others. But being mindful of all of them will strengthen a professional's understanding of ethical concepts and values, enabling more informed ethical decision making.

Golden Mean

Proposed by Aristotle, this perspective *values moderation as a virtue* (Gower 2003). Therefore, the best choice for any situation is the mean or midpoint between two extreme possibilities. For example, in the situation of a product flaw, one extreme would be to keep silent to maintain sales. Another extreme would be to cease production of the product permanently. A midpoint would be to announce a temporary recall until the flaw can be addressed. The theory makes intuitive sense, but a problem can arise in a situation with more nuance and complexity, or it could lead someone to compromise a value-based conviction that would insist on one of the extreme options.

Consequentialist

This perspective, as the name implies, would have an individual *consider the ultimate consequences of a potential action before taking that course* (Gower 2003). If it seems simplistic, think of the many public relations crises that get attention, and the root cause is failure to ask "what might happen" or "who might be offended" or "is there any way this could be misunderstood?" The downside of this approach is that it is not always possible to know what might happen, which is often described as "unforeseen consequences." Nevertheless, envisioning potential and likely consequential harm to others by proposed organizational communication or activity should be standard practice as a matter of both risk management and crisis prevention.

Teleological

Related to the consequentialist view, the *teleological perspective* takes its name from telescope, which means a view to the future. The basis of ethical action in this perspective is consideration of the ends or result, not the means of present action (Bang 2019). The problem with this perspective is it gives rise to the cliché "the ends justify the means," which potentially could lead one to justify cutting ethical corners in the process in order to achieve what can subjectively be considered a good or ethical outcome.

However, many crises occur because of short-term thinking, and a teleological ethical perspective can be a practical means of crisis prevention. Also, a teleological view leads to a mature management strategy in cases where suffering short-term consequences, such as admission of organizational fault or error, results in a long-term positive relationship and reputation.

Utilitarian

The *utilitarian perspective* stresses usefulness, or utility (Gower 2003). A phrase that is often used to explain this perspective is "the greatest good for the greatest number." In other words, the guide to an ethical decision is a mathematical determination of ensuring that a majority of people benefit as a result of the decision a professional has to make. This method is helpful when a public relations professional is faced with an inevitable disagreement between competing stakeholder groups.

A criticism of this perspective, however, is that it can lead to a cold and calculating ethical framework in which a minority opinion is disregarded and its proponents potentially harmed. There are cases where the ethical or "right" thing to do may favor a minority. An example could be when a local government enacts "eminent domain" (seizing with compensation but not with the will of people) to take over the farms of a few families that have had them for generations because a burgeoning community wants a new shopping mall. Or a company may build a factory and tout majority public opinion is in favor because of new jobs and a boost to the economy. A smaller number of residents may oppose it owing to the increase in traffic, environmental harm, or other concerns. Working toward a compromise or accommodating specific concerns would be a wiser strategy and ethically better than simply declaring the majority benefit.

Deontological

The *deontological ethical perspective* places an emphasis on duty. Promoted during the Enlightenment era by German philosopher Immanuel Kant, the theory would have someone consider relationship and responsibility to others prior to the objectives of themselves or those they represent (Bang 2019). The theory also includes the concept of "categorical imperative," which means that if something is ethical in one context, it must be so universally. This lends itself positively to the notion of ethical integrity or consistency of values and actions.

A critique of this perspective is that it can be too rigid and discount other factors when making ethical decisions in varied contexts or cultures. A good general application of this theory is for professionals to ask themselves and the management of those they represent to whom they have a duty and what precisely is that duty in a situation. This makes ethical decisions more authentic and human and not simply blind rule following.

Situational

To counter the idea of a categorical imperative or universal ethics, the *situational approach* notes that love, happiness, and human welfare are the few universal ethical values across cultures. However, other values may vary by situation and culture, and, hence, the need to make "situationally" dependent ethical decisions that weigh unique factors in each case (Gower 2003). The benefit of this approach is responsiveness to specifics of an environment, campaign specifics, or certain publics. But a criticism is that it can lead to moral relativism and justification of bad ethics with a vague referral to the specifics of a situation. This can seem like paying lip service to ethics. A good method to ensure pure intent is to apply other ethical theories and principles to each situation to ensure actions align with objective ethical concerns. This helps avoid subjective interpretation of a situation such that ethics becomes secondary to organizational objective.

These long-standing ethical perspectives have stood the test of time and are still relevant today. Again, they can be seen as contradictory, especially in the case of situational ethics, as opposed to the notion of a categorical imperative. It is helpful to see them not as competing or right or wrong ethical views but as a set of multiple and valid things to think about when striving to be an ethical professional.

The next chapter builds on this set of foundational ethical concepts for all individuals and explains some of the ethical theories and concepts specifically applicable to the professional practice of public relations.

CHAPTER 13

Ethical Theory Specific to Public Relations

Public relations is a broad and diverse field, given the many areas of practice and contexts. The theories in this section integrate foundational ethical philosophies with the practice and even the essence of the public relations profession. Becoming knowledgeable about these theories could help a public relations professional see their role, both in their organization and in society, from a wider lens. It will also equip public relations professionals to counsel management across the organization to make ethical decisions and in the process, to demonstrate more completely and accurately how public relations is a management function.

Ethic of Care

While ethics is often about the character of an individual, the *ethic of care* is based on nurturing relationships. It assumes the heart of public relations practice is creating relationships and facilitating dialogue, trust, and collaboration. It relates to baseline ethics philosophy that considers human flourishing the primary outcome of ethics. Theoretically, the ethic of care should embrace these aspects of public relations and enable them in all aspects of practice: "The ethic of care asserts that human flourishing relies on mutually beneficial relationships" (Lemon and Bowman 2022, 3).

Additionally, the ethic of care is more about responsibilities of the practitioner than the rights of various people. It is about the public relations professional "fulfilling conflicting responsibilities to different people rather than resolving claims of conflicting rights among them" (Simola 2003, 354). This, of course, presents challenges for a public relations professional. The strategy is to make any complaining public aware of competing interests and the organization's responsibility to them as well.

It is about raising the level of discussion beyond a single organization–public relationship and getting people to see the big picture of complex multiple relationships.

Scholars have developed a series of phases in a relationship where the ethic of care is enacted. They are associated with political science but can be applied to public relations as well. The first four phases stressed moral boundaries (Tronto 1993), and a fifth was later added to make explicit the responsibility to maintain care (Western Political Science Association 2013):

1. Caring about—being attentive to the publics' needs;
2. Caring for—meeting the needs identified in phase 1;
3. Care giving—the act of providing care;
4. Care receiving—being reflective, allowing collaboration of caregiver and receiver, finding mutual meaning in action; and
5. Caring with—allow for feedback, build trust and solidarity, provide ongoing care and engagement and not just episodic actions.

Public relations professionals can interpret care from their professional role in several ways. It could mean giving voice to an otherwise unheard public or stakeholder, either to management or the public at large. It could mean providing information requested, not just that which meets the objectives of the organization. It could mean changing the wording of communication in order to be inoffensive. It could mean changing a corporate policy to address potential harm done to a stakeholder. The key is to take the initiative to start with step one and actively listen to publics to know what type of care is needed.

Stakeholder Theory

Stakeholder theory, as an ethical theory, came about as a strategic imperative for management in a capitalist society (Freeman 1984). It is defined as

> a view of capitalism that stresses the interconnected relationships between a business and its customers, suppliers, employees, investors, communities and others who have a stake in the organization.

The theory argues that a firm should create value for all stakeholders, not just shareholders (Stakeholder Theory n.d.).

The theory elevates the need to balance economic and ethical interests of a corporation, although it can easily also be applied to nonprofit organizations whose stakeholders include donors, volunteers, people served, and more. Stakeholders are, essentially, people with whom relationships could be affected, positively or negatively, by operations and achievement of organizational goals, as well as those on whom the organization depends for success. In stakeholder theory, organizations are seen to be interdependent with their publics, more specifically called stakeholders, and "each of the stakeholder interests need to be managed tactfully" (Dzage and Pierog 2023, 157).

The theory is normative in nature because of its assumption that morals, values, and codes of conduct should undergird business operations. It is related to the social pressure on organizations to contribute to improving social good and achieving sustainability.

The application of stakeholder theory for public relations professionals is to see, and encourage management and clients to see, the relationship between organization and publics as more than transactional or about meeting only organizational objectives. Seeing publics as stakeholders who have as much to gain or lose from organizational operations will potentially change the perspective of the very nature and purpose of public relations practice and will likely ensure that it will be more organically ethical.

Legitimacy Theory

In the past decade, there has been a significant increase in the number of organizations—in the corporate, nonprofit, and government sectors—who do sustainability reporting. An advanced form of this is ESG reporting, which means to report how an organization is working to be sustainable in terms of environmental, social, and governance metrics. *Legitimacy theory* is in part behind this emphasis.

The idea behind the theory is that organizations need to earn the right to operate, and they earn that right by being perceived by society as legitimate. Legitimacy in this case means the right to exist in the first place as well as the right to conduct business or pursue a mission. This has also been called a "social license to operate" or SLO (Hamm et al. 2022).

The concept of legitimacy theory emerged from the mining industry when Jim Cooney, the former director of Placer Dam, used such language for the first time in reflecting on the practices of the industry needing local support. He phrased legitimacy as "acceptability of company projects or operations by the neighboring community" (Cooney 2017).

The development of the theory led to a model diagram and set of propositions. The model originated in the field of criminal justice and had a focus on community police but can be extended to public relations and any organization. The diagram is a set of concentric circles with legitimacy at the core, surrounded by authority and acquiescence, which must be balanced. The outer ring includes organizational support, or the perceived ability of the organization to wield power; public approval, the perceived right to wield power; interactions, the evaluations of legal actors; and social context, made up of individual predispositions (Hamm et al. 2022). The diagram is further explained by a set of five propositions:

1. Legitimacy comes from an ongoing dialogue or negotiation of empowerment and reaction of an audience, with an interplay between authority and acquiescence.
2. Support for the organization is required to give it the ability to wield power.
3. Public approval influences authority because the right to wield power is perceptual.
4. Interactions contribute to legitimacy as the public recognizes and responds positively to organizational authority.
5. Individuals have predispositions about power, in general, and the organization, in particular, that contribute to the social context and its influence on whether or not the organization has legitimacy.

Legitimacy theory has been considered normative as well as empirical. Theorists acknowledge that it is a complex concept. However, it is also simple. For public relations professionals, it is similar to asking permission before speaking or acting. They must be mindful that when they act by themselves or on behalf of an organization or client, they may be wielding a form of power that is resented by certain stakeholders. Those who proposed the diagram model and theoretical propositions sum it up succinctly: "In order for power holders to effectively prevent and address social harms, their efforts to assert power with the goal of achieving social influence must be met by the compliance, cooperation and support of their audience" (Hamm et al. 2022, 140).

Moral Judgment/Moral Development Theory

Moral judgment theory is essentially about justice. Justice comes in the form of equality, fairness, and individual rights. Preceding moral judgment are the terms morality, which means cultural structures designed to enable people to live in harmony, and moral development, which means to organize cooperation in society (Myyry 2022).

Moral development is something that is constructed by individuals, not society. Even children make moral judgments independently of adults (Kohlburg 1984). Individuals go through three levels of moral reasoning that are associated with five levels of moral development. At the preconventional level, individuals are at the egocentric and individualistic stages of moral development. At the conventional level, individuals are progressing from stage 3, in which they consider the perspective of close others, and stage 4, which is to weigh a societal point of view. At the postconventional level, individuals take on a moral point of view and give equal consideration to themselves and others. As individuals progress through stages of moral development, the notion of cooperation takes on different meanings. It progresses from simple obedience and doing what they are told, to short-term compliance and deals, to recognition of long-term relationships with familiar persons, to, finally, cooperation with competitors and even those with whom they are not familiar. At the highest level of moral development, all perspectives in a moral judgment are coordinated (Kohlburg 1984). It is easy to see how this moral development in terms of relational cooperation is consonant with a progression from a fundamental to more ethically enlightened view of public relations. Moral judgment theory is also related to contingency theory, which will be discussed in Part VI in the context of crisis communications (Xu et al. 2023).

Moral foundation theory is another way of explaining how people vary in their moral judgment. People have six innate moral foundations that affect their personal moral judgment. Each of the foundations is a place on a scale that enables people to make gut reactions about patterns in the world to see as right or wrong or to like or dislike something. Again, ethics is not always black and white. So most people's foundations would be between an ethical ideal and an obviously unethical posture. The foundations are as follows:

1. Care/harm;
2. Fairness/cheating;
3. Loyalty/betrayal;
4. Authority/subversion;
5. Sanctity/degradation; and
6. Liberty/oppression (Graham et al. 2013).

Public relations professionals can apply the theory to themselves and consider their own moral development and moral foundations. These would be primary internal influences on their moral judgment that affect ethical decisions they make as professionals. Another way to apply the theory is to consider the moral development level and moral foundations of publics to whom they will be communicating. Actions should be adjusted to be consistent with what publics perceive as ethical.

Corporate Social Responsibility/Advocacy Theory

In recent years, companies and their leadership getting publicly engaged in social issues and causes has gone from unusual to uniform, from a brand distinction to a public expectation. The practical and theoretical terms for this phenomenon are corporate social responsibility (CSR) and Corporate Social Advocacy (CSA). CSR is about conducting business in a responsible way by not harming people or the environment in the course of regular operations. CSA goes a step further and involves championing a social cause, often referred to as "taking a stand" on social issues. There has been much discussion about how to be responsible, how to communicate responsibility, which causes and how many to support, and how to demonstrate advocacy. Theory specific to CSR and CSA is still emerging. Previous studies and theoretical concepts can be applied to CSR in a way that gives theoretical guidance to strategically selecting and communicating about CSR activities. Meanwhile, the existing moral foundations theory and balance theory mentioned previously has been used to form a new proposed theory specific to CSA. That will be discussed further on, but CSA can best be understood in the context of CSR since it evolved from it.

Companies that practice CSR routinely communicate about their ethical values and responsible behavior. This can be done in annual reports, sustainability reports, and diversity reports as well as news releases, advertising, websites, and other tactics. The hope is not just to show accountability for claims of responsibility but to improve public recognition and brand reputation. CSR activities could be changes in policy, product ingredients, hiring practices, or any number of significant operational changes that reflect a more responsible approach to business that leads to the benefit of society. However, communicating CSR actions does not always lead to positive public recognition and can also lead to skepticism and rejection of the communication efforts. Therefore, the question is not whether CSR efforts are shared but how (Vilagra et al. 2016).

The solution comes from the distinction between two types of "fit" for CSR actions. Fit is a concept, not a theory, that has emerged from many prior studies about CSR and communication. Personal fit is the perception of publics that a company's CSR actions are relevant to themselves personally. Meanwhile, corporate fit refers to a logical coherence or link between a company's normal corporate activities or product category and its CSR activities. In an experimental study, corporate fit messages were as persuasive as a control message. Personal fit messages led to a higher level of perceived sincerity and honesty. This speaks to strategy in terms of both the kinds of CSR activities selected and the way they are communicated:

> Companies should ensure that CSR actions are sufficiently aligned with normal business operations that the public will perceive them as competent in their social engagement. At the same time—and potentially to an even greater extent—companies should ensure that CSR actions resonate personally with stakeholders (Vilagra et al. 2016, 143).

As noted, CSA comes with a greater risk of alienating stakeholders than does CSR. This is because the requisite support or opposition to social issues means entering into a controversial and divisive subject. Some CSA has led to a significant measure of success in terms of corporate recognition and reputation, which has translated into other business metrics such as sales, investment, and employee satisfaction and recruitment. Other CSA efforts have backfired to the extent that it caused significant reputational and monetary damage, or they attracted some publics but alienated others.

For this reason, scholars have sought to develop a *theory of corporate social advocacy (CSA) success* to give clear guidance to professionals planning and communicating CSA (Parcha 2024). The theory is based on moral foundations theory and balance theory mentioned previously. Recall that there are six moral dimensions in moral foundations theory, each with two polar opposites such as care/harm. Balance theory asserts that people prefer relationships in which there is a balance or agreement and harmony. These two theories, taken with research that shows CSA must be perceived as authentic to be believed and appreciated, form the basis of a proposed theory of CSA success.

In this theory, success is defined as the "stakeholders' aggregated favorability toward the CSA" (Parcha 2024, 3). The theory offers a formula combining the theoretical constructs described previously that are the practical takeaway for professionals: CSA success is achieved by the combination of emphasizing the correct moral foundation, taking a stance that stakeholders agree with, and being authentic in advocating for a particular issue (Parcha 2024). Concepts of fit from aforementioned CSR research would lead to a perception of authenticity. It is important to realize that the definition of success accounts for "aggregated" stakeholder favorability—sometimes, a choice must be made to appeal to some stakeholders even as others may not agree. That decision should be made judiciously in terms of benefit and cost to the organization.

Dialogue and Ethics

Dialogue was addressed earlier when discussing digital communication. But dialogue also exists offline and can be facilitated in all forms of communication. Theoretically, a theory of dialogue within public relations' larger body of theories is useful. But some say that dialogue is the essence of public relations itself: "The goal of public relations is to manage communications in a way that comes as close as possible to dialogue. This is the core ethical responsibility from which all other obligations follow" (Pearson 1989, 128).

If dialogue is central to public relations practice, it is worthwhile considering the true meaning of dialogue theoretically. It has been said to occur when two parties communicating are both able to move from one level of abstraction to another (Habermas, 1984). Others have expanded on that description to offer four specific requirements for dialogue:

1. Both parties have an equal chance to initiate and maintain discourse;
2. Both parties have an equal chance to make challenges, explanations, and interpretations;
3. The interaction is free of manipulation, domination, or control; and
4. Participants are equal with respect to power (Burleson and Kline 1979).

True dialogue in an interaction is characterized by agreement among participants. Theorists have identified six specific dimensions on which participants must agree for there to be dialogue. There should be agreement on the following:

1. The rules for beginning, maintaining, and ending an interaction;
2. The time separating messages or questions from answers;
3. The opportunities to suggest or change topics;
4. When a response counts as a response;
5. The selection of a channel in which to interact; and
6. Talking about and changing rules (Pearson 1989).

Public relations professionals should learn from this that dialogue is not just any interaction, nor is it even a two-way interaction. There is clearly more to it than that. Professionals who seek to establish true dialogue will be engaging in advanced and ethical public relations practice. They can show that dialogue is not a feature but the essence of public relations and in so doing, demonstrate that public relations practiced properly is inherently ethical.

Diversity and Ethics

Along with CSR and CSA, *diversity* has gained considerable attention in all organizations and in the profession of public relations, in particular. Theorists require that terms or concepts be defined, and public relations has not yet offered a common definition of diversity. Discussions of diversity have tended to focus on race and sexual orientation. However, religion, socioeconomic status, geographic origin, education, and other factors are equally important (Wills 2020).

While the term diversity has not been universally defined, public relations scholars have offered normative theoretical proposals linking diversity to public relations practice. Interviews with high-ranking public relations professionals on the subject have led to best practice recommendations that diversity should be embedded in practice from communication planning to building organizational culture. Foundational to public relations and diversity is the ethical mandate to listen to and ask questions of all stakeholders. Based on all of this reasoning, a diversity-driven public relations model has been proposed that includes paying attention and having honest conversations; embedding diversity in the culture from leadership to programs; being explicit in communication messages about why diversity is relevant and matters to the organization; and selecting the best messengers for each message with diversity in mind (Mundy 2015).

Further theoretical development in the area of diversity and public relations practice could happen given that public relations—with its multistakeholder view—is well suited to leading diversity in organizations. It has been proposed that such theory look at diversity both structurally and culturally. Internal structures could reflect diversity in terms of networking, training, and programming. External structures facilitating diversity would include recruitment and retention as well as making a business case for diversity. Culturally, an organization would show diversity internally by treating employees as individuals and having a diverse source of learning for organizational change. Externally, a culturally diverse organization would engage diverse communities and use public relations' advocacy role to engage in social justice (Mundy 2015). Public relations professionals should consider diversity not just a cultural demand but an organizational necessity. Diversity should be seen through a communicative lens in terms of individual needs for information and expression from a variety of perspectives. Also, public relations professionals are well suited to leading or co-leading such efforts given the profession's multistakeholder perspective. However, corporate oversight of diversity as well as CSR and ESG initiatives is often managed by board or staff members who are from functions other than public relations. Sometimes, these individuals have degrees and job titles or head committees specific to diversity or sustainability (Penning 2024). Professionals in public relations will need to take the initiative and be assertive to claim in practice what is theoretically a public relations role of managing diversity.

It should also be acknowledged that just as with ethics, generally, there is a diversity of opinions and perspectives—or we could say theories—about diversity. There has been some public pushback against DEI (diversity, equity, inclusion) programs. However, this is most often an objection to DEI specifically as a set of claims and proposals and not diversity generally as a concept. That is because in many cases, DEI manifests itself in ways that reflect the Marxist origins of critical race theory, which views issues through a polar lens of oppressor versus victim, and this singular but not universal construct has permeated many institutions (Rufo 2023). One key player in propagating this theory of diversity is Angela Davis, a student of Herbert Marcuse of the Marxist perspective Frankfurt School in Germany, who designed a curriculum based on Vladimir Lenin, Malcolm X, Frantz Fanon, and Che Guevara to "reset the entire oppressive structure of America" (from Davis's own words in documents at the University of California San Diego). Notably, with regard to the spread of DEI, the stated first objective of Davis' new theory was to establish racial and sexual identities as a basis for political action (Rufo 2023). However, this bespeaks ideological activism more than theoretical proposition.

Meanwhile, research has shown that DEI has failed to improve diversity. The Heritage Foundation has pointed this out in a commentary on its website:

> Diversity training programs have failed to improve attitudes and behaviors for years and attempts to reduce bias through measuring just how much each of us has stored away in the recesses of our mind have been a spectacular bust. Anthropology Now reports that hundreds of studies dating back to the 1930s suggest that anti-bias training doesn't reduce bias (Butcher 2023).

The National Association of Scholars has determined that bias training hijacks justice (Randall 2024). Studies by the Rutgers University Social Perception Lab and the Network Contagion Research Institute found that DEI training causes people to find racism where none exists (Jagdeep et al. 2024).

A growing number of Black intellectuals have also been critical of the particulars of some DEI assertions and prescriptions and offered their own alternatives:

- Carol Swain, co-author of "The Adversity of Diversity" and a prominent Black political science professor, recently retired, labels DEI programs an "aggressive force that takes organizations away from their core missions and often transforms them into divisive and disruptive institutions that openly violate the rights of members of disfavored groups" (Swain and Towle 2023). Swain's recommended solution of Real Unity Training Solutions (https://unitytrainingsolutions.com/) entails a return to core American principles that embrace nondiscrimination and equal opportunity in a meritocratic system that recognizes individual effort rather than group rights.
- John McWhorter details how claims to 'dismantle racist structures' is actually harming his fellow Black Americans by infantilizing Black people, setting Black students up for failure, and passing policies that disproportionately damage Black

communities. What is called 'antiracism' actually features a racial essentialism that's barely distinguishable from racist arguments of the past (McWhorter 2021).

- Shelby Steele, a Black *New York Times* columnist, argues that our culture has been trapped in putting color before character or considering only racial categories and not individual attributes (Steele 1998).
- Coleman Hughes, a young Black intellectual, argues for a return to the ideals that inspired the American Civil Rights movement, showing how our departure from the color-blind ideal has ushered in a new era of fear, paranoia, and resentment marked by draconian interpersonal etiquette, failed corporate diversity and inclusion efforts, and poisonous race-based policies that hurt the very people they intend to help (Hughes 2024).
- Robert Woodson, a contemporary of Rev. Dr. Martin Luther King in the civil rights movement, founded the Woodson Center (www.woodsoncenter.org) to help underserved communities fight crime and violence and restore families by applying the principles of market economy, faith, and personal responsibility. Woodson also edited the book *Red, White and Black: Rescuing American History from Revisionists and Race Hustlers*, which features prominent Black scholars telling the story of Black people "living the grand American experience, however bumpy the road may be along the way" (Woodson 2021).

While not everyone will agree with the foregoing authors and organizations on the subject of diversity, it is important for both theory and practice to acknowledge multiple perspectives, particularly from those whom diversity programs claim to help. Public relations professionals should certainly seek to engage in diversity initiatives for reasons articulated previously, but they should first listen to all publics specific to their organization and be judicious and strategic when determining the methods by which they will work to encourage diversity.

CHAPTER 14

Professional Ethical Decision-Making Models

The theories so far in this chapter are useful to help professionals develop a framework for thinking and acting ethically. But the final section of this chapter is most practical because it lists some models for ethical decision making, which are stepwise processes to ensure thorough consideration of all factors in an ethical decision in order to make a decision and act with professional confidence and a clear conscience. The chapter concludes with a discussion of codes of ethics and the concept of developing ethical organizational cultures. The models share some similar concepts and steps, but each offers some distinctive differences as well. All should be useful in providing a process for strategic thinking about ethical practice as compared with feeling uncertainty, acting on gut instinct, or being reduced to justifying behavior that is ethically questionable but not specifically illegal.

Potter Box

The *Potter Box* was developed by Ralph Potter, a professor at the Harvard Divinity School. This is a four-step process for ethical decision making:

1. Define the ethical issue or determine the facts at play in a situation.
2. Identify the values of all people involved that should be employed.
3. Recognize the guiding ethics principles that apply in the situation.
4. Ascertain the loyalties in the situation or the people to whom one has responsibility (Arthur W. Page Center 2024).

TARES

The *TARES model* is a focus not only on decision making but also on ethical persuasion. It is a process stated in the form of an acronym, in which each is an element of persuasion that can be considered ethical:

- Truthfulness—of the message.
- Authenticity—of the persuader.
- Respect—for the public being persuaded.
- Equity—of the persuasive appeal; it is not one-sided.
- Social responsibility—persuasion advances or does not harm the common good (Baker and Mortinson 2001).

Bowen's Model for Ethical Decision Making

Ethics scholar Shannon Bowen has developed an *Ethical Decision-Making Model* that also adds an element of strategy. The model includes three steps and a visual triangular model. The steps are as follows:

1. Ensure the professional is autonomous (able to think and act independently);
2. Consider key duties to the client and the public when making decisions; and
3. Consider the relevant ethical questions when communicating the choice (Bowen 2005).

The triangular model shows the interaction of three considerations and is based on the deontological concept of duty. The top of the "Ethical Consideration Triangle" is duty and calls on a professional to consider their duty to self, society, publics/stakeholders, and the organization. Another corner of the triangle is intention, which would mean a professional ensures they are acting with moral goodwill. The last corner of the triangle is ensuring that dignity and respect for others is maintained (Bowen 2005, 173).

Moral Development Model

A decision-making model that focuses on an individual's level of morality applies *moral development theory*. The model has four steps:

1. Moral recognition or awareness. A person sees a moral or ethical issue.
2. Use of moral reasoning to decide ethical action.
3. Moral intent, an act of prioritizing ethical values above personal values, empowering a desire to do what is right.
4. Moral behavior, or following through on intent (Rest 1986).

PRSA Six-Step Ethical Decision-Making Model

The Public Relations Society of America (PRSA) offers professionals a six-step guide to making ethical decisions in the course of practice:

1. Define the specific ethical issue or conflict.
2. Identify internal and external factors (e.g., legal, political, social, economic) that may influence the decision.
3. Identify key ethical values that apply to the situation.
4. Identify the publics who will be affected by the decision, and identify the public relations' professionals' obligation to each.
5. Select ethical principles to guide the decision-making process.
6. Make a decision and justify it (Fitzpatrick, n.d.).

Again, the models have some areas of overlap and some distinctions. The overlap gives validity to the processes as confirmed by multiple scholars. Professionals can find one that works best or select different decision-making models for different ethical questions. Some professionals and organizations also adapt their own ethical decision-making process with specific people to be involved and questions to ask given their unique organizational culture or industry setting. Such ethical processes could be formalized in a policy manual, such as employee handbooks or crisis communication plans, to give ethical decision making concrete value.

It is worth noting that among the common elements of each model is a requisite first step of *identifying* the ethical issue. This requires some knowledge of ethics because potential ethical violations are not always obvious. A professional may sense that something does not seem right, but being able to articulate something specific—a conflict of interest, not acknowledging the needs or concerns of a particular public, not sharing all relevant information—is a vital step to ensuring that the response is both relevant and ethically appropriate.

In the same way, the models all call for *applying* values. This speaks to the ethical concepts illuminated in the ethical theories from classical to industry specific. Being fluent in the language of ethical values, and matching them to organizational statements of value and purpose (see the section on culture that follows), makes ethical navigation much easier in terms of knowing what to do and having the support of leadership and others in the organization, as well as developing a reputation based on ethical perspective and behavior.

Codes of Ethics and Ethical Culture

Codes of ethics are common to have for individual organizations and professional trade associations. Their value is to provide a visual commitment to ethics and to offer some guidance to professionals who desire to do the right thing, as well as putting the brakes on actions or communications that are potentially unethical.

Codes of ethics have also been criticized theoretically. From a postmodern, theoretical perspective, codes of ethics have a diminishing effect on ethical behavior because people outsource their own critical thinking. This view rejects codes of ethics in favor of individual decision making that can reflect unique environments and the situation of the practitioner and makes professionals more intimately engaged with ethics, as opposed to peripheral compliance with a generalized guideline (Holtzhausen 2015).

Other scholars have taken a more compromised view on codes of ethics from a theoretical position. A review of professional public relations associations in 107 countries helped to determine that some ethical standards are universal while others are contextual. So codes can include those ethical concepts that are generalized but also leave room for practitioners to use their own judgment in specific contexts. The universal ethical values include honesty, safeguarding confidences of clients, and prohibiting conflicts of interest. Other ethical issues such as the free flow of information, fees, and gifts are more relativistic ethical values that could vary by culture (Kim and Ki 2014).

Several professional organizations (e.g., not solely academics) have put forth practical standards of public relations practice that are ethical and universal in a global context. The Global Alliance issued its Melbourne Mandate after a forum in Melbourne Australia to assert that public relations professionals have a mandate to define and maintain an organization's character and values, build a culture of listening and engagement, and instill responsible behaviors by individuals and organizations. The full document includes more specific responsibilities and ways public relations professionals can fulfill this mandate. It incorporates many of the theoretical ethics concepts from this chapter (Global Alliance 2012).

Similarly, the International Public Relations Association (IPRA) has a code of conduct to guide professionals in public relations operating across the globe that includes 18 specific ethical situations with guidance (International Public Relations Association 2020).

Just as was noted with respect to diversity, some argue that ethics should be embedded in culture and not reduced to a code. The idea is that ethics should permeate all practice and should be second nature and not an occasional reference to a code. The PR Council, an association of public relations firms, has produced an "Ethics as Culture" resource guide to help professionals ensure that agencies and their client organizations develop and maintain organizational cultures in which ethics is a primary value (Public Relations Council 2024).

Professionals should not necessarily rule out considering industry codes of ethics or developing their own organizational code of conduct owing to criticism of codes. But good practice would be to have a code as well as build an ethical culture. The code can be a foundation, and it can be used in onboarding, training, and other aspects of organizational operations and communication to make ethics something embedded and not only occasionally referenced.

Strategic Summary of Part V—Ethics

Ethics is often considered to be a weight on strategy or a limit on public relations success. But the opposite is true. In a society in which communication is fast, transparent, and shared, being ethical is a wise strategy that not only prevents crisis but contributes to understanding, agreement, and positive relationships. In that context, many specific public relations and organizational goals are more likely to be achieved. Ancient to modern ethical theories and the variety of practical decision-making models give public relations professionals food for thought as they guide organizations to do what is right as well as successful.

- Good ethics is good strategy for long-term positive relationship and reputation building.
- Sometimes, the right ethical path is not one or the other but the mean between the two.
- Considering the largest number who will benefit may be the ethical way so long as the decision does not significantly harm the minority.
- Professionals should weigh the duty they have to all stakeholders and seek to be consistent in fulfilling that duty, but this ethical posture should be authentic and not just conform to a rigid rule.
- Situational ethics has the advantage of considering nuances of a specific situation or publics and may lead to the most ethical decision on a case-by-case basis, but it could be abused by professionals who rationalize ethically suspect behavior to meet organizational or personal goals.
- An ethic of care would require professionals to start by being attentive to publics' needs and not just their response to organizational initiatives. This should include otherwise unheard publics.
- An ethical posture for any organization is to see itself as interdependent with its various stakeholders and to manage the unique interests of each stakeholder carefully.

- Organizations should seek permission from publics to operate, or legitimacy, by dialogue and not simply assert its own legal rights.
- Theoretical research has shown that people have six moral foundation scales. Professionals should apply this to themselves and their organizations to determine where they stand and also consider the moral foundations of their publics respectfully when communicating with them.
- Success in CSA comes from emphasizing the right moral foundation, taking the stance that stakeholders agree with, and being authentic when advocating for a particular issue.
- Real dialogue is dependent on publics and organizations agreeing on a variety of conditions for communicating and equal power in the interaction.
- Diversity as an ethical concept is a matter of both organizational structure and culture.
- While there are several ethical decision-making models, they have in common a knowledge and application of ethical concepts and values from theory.
- Codes of ethics, whether from outside sources or an organization's own, can be useful but may also remove individuals from thinking critically about each ethical situation.
- Developing an organizational ethical culture can be a good strategy to make ethics embedded and organic and not an afterthought.

PART VI

Public Relations Theories: The Management Perspective

Public relations draws theory from other professions and academic domains and has little theory if its own. That is actually good for the field because "it makes professional knowledge adaptable, layered, and dynamic" (Bowman and Hendy 2019, 339). Theory applied to public relations could come from communications, sociology, psychology, management, or many other fields, as has been demonstrated in previous chapters. One review of research in public relations determined that 87 different theories were applied to public relations practice (Meadows and Meadows 2014). In recent years, public relations scholars have generated more theory specific to the field. That is the focus of this section. The relevant theories are organized into categories about practice models, the roles of a practitioner, and, finally, theories about relationship and engagement.

CHAPTER 15

Models and Dimensions of Public Relations Practice

As public relations grew as a formal profession, theorists and professionals alike sought to understand how it was practiced and to propose best ways to practice. What follows is a blend of normative and empirical models and theories that have emerged and developed over time to guide public relations practice and encourage a standard process and characteristics of good practice worthy of being called a profession.

Grunig's Four Models of Public Relations

Based on observations and interviews with large numbers of professionals, as well as critical thinking about public relations practice, a typology of models of public relations practice was developed and has often been cited by academics and professionals to this day (Grunig 1989). The four models of practice do show a historical development as public relations became more advanced in purpose and function. However, all four models are evident even today and practiced in different organizations or over time in the same organization in different situations. The first two models are considered forms of one-way communication.

- *Press Agentry/Publicity*—this model comes from the early days, in the 1900s, when "press agents" or "publicity men" was the name for those who sought media attention. Unfortunately, this practice was associated with attention seeking by any means and considered stunts or propaganda. Some public relations professionals today are focused on media relations and publicity, or it is at least a part of their responsibility or campaign strategy to gain earned media. Most today would frown on gimmicks and stunts in seeking publicity.

- *Public Information*—this model is a more ethically evolved form of practice that still seeks media attention but does so honestly. Also, public information may involve using other tactics such as advertising or brochures to inform the public. The focus was on honest information. Ivy Lee, a pioneer of public relations practice credited with being the first to use a "press release," offered a set of principles distinguishing public information from press agentry and characterized it as honest (Penning 2008). This model may have given rise to the characterization of public relations "putting an organization in a positive light" because professionals in this model would not volunteer negative information. Today, it is common for a public relations professional to be called a public information officer (PIO) consistent with this model. This is most often in government agencies or taxpayer-funded organizations that have an obligation to provide information to citizens.

The next two practice models exhibit two-way communication.

- *Two-Way Asymmetrical*—in this model, professionals use research to determine the best way to gain public support, as well as following up to see if their campaigns had a desired impact on the public. In other words, professionals are concerned with tailoring messages and measuring responses in attitude and behavior, as opposed to merely seeing resulting mentions in the news media. The asymmetry means that the two-way only implies understanding publics enough to communicate strategically to them and to measure their response (Message → Public → Response). It emphasizes gaining public support or change without the organization changing its own behavior.
- *Two-Way Symmetrical*—this model is also two-way but more completely so. Professionals who practice public relations in this way seek symmetry with publics in the form of mutual understanding and benefit, which means professionals engage not just in communicating and monitoring but also

in bargaining, negotiating, and conflict resolution. It closely follows the Shannon and Weaver model of communication discussed earlier. This model of practice therefore means that an organization itself could adapt based on relationships with publics. Therefore, this model of practice could "bring symbiotic changes in ideas, attitudes and behaviors of both the organization and its publics" (Grunig 1989, 29).

Professionals could look honestly at their own or their agency/ department public relations practice using these models and dimensions and see if it matches the context or if they could intentionally aspire to a different type of practice. This could lead to changes in their sense of the profession and their own mission and value in their organization, which could ultimately be the case that theory leads to positive adjustments in practice. While these models were observed and proposed long before the Internet, they can be seen in public relations professionals' engagement on social media in ways ranging from attention seeking to more genuine symmetrical relational styles. The four models could also be seen as stages in a campaign, and professionals can ethically adjust messages based on public response at each stage to determine message acceptance and even sharing by intended publics. This is consistent with the B.A.S.I.C. model, addressed previously (Michaelson and Stacks 2011).

RACE, RPIE, ROSTE, and ROPES

In addition to models of practice, a set of similar public relations practice processes were developed. They vary slightly in nomenclature but are similar overall in terms of the specific activities a public relations professional should do in sequence for effective practice.

The *RACE* process stands for research, action plan, communication, and evaluation. Research includes identifying and segmenting relevant publics for a given campaign. The action plan includes setting measurable outcome objectives, determining strategies and tactics that deliver those objectives, and including a timeline and budget. The evaluation step in the process looks back at the stated objectives to see if the desired changes in public awareness, attitude, or action were achieved. Another acronym for this process is RPIE, which stands for research, planning, implementation, and evaluation (Marsten 1963).

The *ROSTE* process, a slight modification of RACE, is research, objectives, strategies, tactics, and evaluation. It is similar to RACE but highlights objectives and strategies from the action plan and states tactics instead of communication.

The *ROPES* process also starts with research and continues with objectives but then adds planning and execution. This makes objectives paramount and precedes the planning and execution states. The added concept in this model is stewardship, which means to maintain relationships beyond the campaign (Marsten 1963). The stewardship aspect of this process involves four ways to foster relationships—reciprocity, responsibility, reporting, and relational nurturing. Reciprocity means showing gratitude to stakeholders. Responsibility means keeping promises made to stakeholders. Reporting means updating publics about issues for which they initially sought support or were solicited to respond. And, finally, relational nurturing simply means using multiple forms of communication that have the objective of relationship and not just a response to the organizational goals (Waters 2009).

It has been found that the process may be consistent, in general, but the specifics may vary by practice area or context. For example, professionals may have different specific publics in corporate, nonprofit, government, sports, tourism, investor relations, consumer relations, and so on. This will lead to necessary variance in what information is sought and the method of finding it in research, as well as different specific objectives and related strategies and tactics. But while the specific applications necessarily vary, the general outline of these processes is consistent and useful for public relations practice (Penning 2012).

Professionals can certainly apply any process model they prefer. The key is to avoid a mindset of celebrating attractive tactics and resulting attention of unclear value to the organization. A good practice model gives confidence when it is based on research and not instinct. Research also feeds into strategy by tailoring public relations to understand publics and problems. Setting and measuring *outcome* objectives (i.e., how the identified publics respond, not just what the public relations professional did) is more likely to be effective and show the value of public relations to management and clients.

Excellence Theory

While practice models are normative suggestions for good practice, public relations scholars also wanted a way to demonstrate the best quality of practice. The goal was to have a broad general theory of public relations based on multiple midlevel theories that had emerged (Grunig and Grunig, 2006). Research in public relations began in the 1950s as an offshoot of mass communication research. In time, the understanding of the essence of public relations went beyond communication to be considered a management function, but "many people years later continue to think of public relations as publicity or media relations" (Grunig and Grunig 2006, 23).

The well-known "excellence study" was conducted in response to this diminished conception of the growing field of public relations. Based on interviews with members of the International Association of Business Communicators (IABC), the study resulted in a book that sought to answer three questions: 1. When are the efforts of communication professionals effective? 2. How do organizations benefit from effective public relations? 3. Why do organizations practice public relations in different ways? "The three questions are of great theoretical interest to researchers, but they may be of even greater potential practical concern to working public relations professionals" who have to defend their program to management (Grunig 1992, 1).

Excellence theory made the distinction between effective and excellent, the latter meaning that it contributes to organizational effectiveness. Characteristics of "excellent" public relations were determined at different levels. At the program level, for individual public relations programs, they were managed strategically and evaluated outcomes, not just outputs.

The department or functional level refers to structure and process. At this level, excellence is demonstrated by having a single or integrated public relations department that does not report to marketing or another function, such as development in a nonprofit setting. The senior public relations person, who should be a manager and not a technician (see roles theory in Chapter 17), reports directly to senior management and is part of the dominant coalition, those people in the organization who make decisions. An excellent public relations department practices the two-way symmetrical model and embeds diversity in all PR roles.

Finally, excellent public relations can be reflected at the overall organizational level. The management worldview or perception of what public relations is should be consistent with two-way symmetrical practice. The culture should be participative rather than authoritarian. The organizational structure is organic rather than mechanical, with symmetrical internal communications and high employee job satisfaction.

The original questions that preceded the study that led to excellence theory were about how organizations benefit from excellent public relations. The theory asserts that the effects of excellent public relations include programs that meet the objectives of leadership and not just the department; result in a reduced cost of regulation, public pressure and litigation; and generate high job satisfaction among employees (Grunig and Grunig 2006).

Excellent public relations practice also benefits the profession itself:

> The Excellence study has shown that public relations is a unique management function that helps an organization interact with the social and political components of its environment. The value of public relations comes from the relationship that organizations develop and maintain with publics (Grunig and Grunig 2006, 55).

Some have used concepts from excellence theory to address criticisms that the models mentioned previously are not adequate to describe the depth and variety of public relations practice across all contexts. Others said the models failed to account for the relational emphasis in public relations or provide a means to measure effectiveness (Laskin 2012). One proposal was to consider not general models or dimensions of public relations but to view public relations practice on a series of scales that visualize an organization's attitude toward publics and its resulting form of practice. The scales are continuous and range from -10 to $+10$, with an ideal form of practice being on a midpoint. These dimensions include the following:

- The direction of communication. One extreme would be from the organization, and the other would be to the organization. The midpoint would be most reflective of a preferred two-way communication.

- The intended beneficiary scale would show if efforts were in the organization's interest or in the public interest or somewhere in between. A midpoint would reveal a dual interest or a preferred consideration of mutual benefit.
- The strategic nature scale would show whether public relations efforts are reactive or proactive or a mixture. More proactive work reflects a strategic intent.
- The roles scale would reflect whether public relations practice is primarily technical output or managerial concern, managerial being preferred, but some technical roles are obviously necessary.
- The time frame scale would measure whether public relations efforts are focused on short-term goals and practices or work toward long-term collaboration with publics, long-term focus being reflective of a more relational and strategic form of practice (Laskin 2012).

Such scales could be used in communication audits or for CCOs to evaluate and adjust their own practice over time. They could also be used to evaluate the practice of different specializations in public relations, such as investor relations compared with consumer relations. Comparisons could also be made using these scales to compare public relations as practiced in different regions, nations, or cultures.

Apart from the scales, public relations professionals can apply aspects of the robust excellence theory in several ways. They can work to become part of management or the dominant coalition to help make organizational decisions, based on the multistakeholder view of public relations, as opposed to merely communicating them. They can work to set objectives that meet management and organizational objectives and measure the outcome of their work to demonstrate that the value of public relations to the overall organization is beyond publicity and other tactical proficiency.

Situational Theory of Publics/Problem Solving

One of the more advanced theories specific to the practice of public relations is the *situational theory of problem* solving (STOPS). It is an extension of the situational theory of publics developed previously. The situational theory of publics had distinguished between active/aware publics and latent/nonpublics. The extended situational theory of problem solving asserts that publics engage with organizations because they have a problem to solve and that professionals should not have a "general" public but specific publics, or they risk failure. This is behind a new concept in the theory, communicative action in problem solving (CAPS), which considers publics as active or passive. CAPS posits that a person with a problem to solve is a more active communicator in terms of information acquisition, selection, and transmission (Kim and Grunig 2011).

STOPS combines variables in the older situational theory of publics with six variables in CAPS to propose a model that explains why and how publics respond to and/or engage with organizations.

The model states that publics are motivated to solve a problem based on four variables, which were part of the situational theory of publics:

- Problem recognition—when what a public expects differs from what they experience, and they sense a problem exists;
- Constraint recognition—people perceive there are obstacles that limit their ability to do anything about a situation;
- Involvement recognition—a person's perceived connection between themself and the problem situation; and
- Referent criterion—any knowledge or subjective judgmental system that influences the way in which a person approaches problem solving (Kim and Grunig 2011).

The levels a person or public has in the preceding four variables will determine the level of their situational motivation for problem solving. This is defined as "a state of cognitive and epistemic readiness to make problem-solving efforts and decrease the perceived discrepancy between expected and experiential states" (Kim and Grunig 2011, 132). Put simply, what a person thinks and knows encourages them to address a perceived problem of not experiencing what they expect from an organization.

The theory states that the higher a person's motivation to solve a problem, the more likely they are to engage in communicative action to solve their problem (CAPS). There are six outcomes—theoretically variables—from someone being motivated to communicate, and they are in three domains. Each domain has an active or a passive posture, depending on the person's motivation to active communication:

- The domain of acquiring information could have an active response of planned information seeking. The passive response would be attending to information they receive coincidentally.
- The domain of information selection has an active aspect of information forefending, which means a person chooses information that is relative and fends off what is not. A passive response would be information permitting, which is seen in a person accepting any information related to a task.
- The domain of information transmitting has an active posture of information forwarding, in which a person has a proactive, planned, and self-propelled way of sharing information. As an alternative, a passive response to transmitting information would be sharing, which is reactive and done only on request (Kim and Grunig 2011).

What this means simply is that the more a person is committed to resolving a problem, the more likely they are to selectively acquire information relative to that problem and spread it to others. Publics with a higher motivation to communicate with an organization to solve a problem will be more systematic and specific in their communication and focused on relevance of information. Motivated communicators are high in all active and passive behaviors in seeking, selecting, and transmitting information, where passive problem solvers are high only in the passive information behaviors.

Practical application for a public relations professional centers on the variables in this theory and seeing publics not categorically (employees, consumers, etc.) but by the problem they have and their motivation to engage to solve it. Professionals could make their campaign objectives related to the situational variables of seeking, selecting, and sharing information. Strategies and messaging could focus in stimulating problem and involvement recognition, appealing to referent criterion and mitigating constraint recognition. Then, messages could include calls to action to seek and forward information relative to the public's problem that coincides with the topic of a campaign.

CHAPTER 16

Public Relations Professional Roles Theories

Chapter 15 covered theories that relate to how public relations is practiced at the organizational level. This chapter will share theories about roles the individual takes on while practicing public relations. These will cover how public relations professionals conceive of their roles, how other individuals from other professions sometimes usurp or intrude on that role, and how a professional can assess their own competence in public relations.

Role Enactment Theory

Research and theory about public relations roles initially identified four distinct roles of practice. The most sophisticated role was that of an expert prescriber, who would provide counsel to senior management. A communication facilitator serves as a liaison between management and key publics. A problem-solving facilitator develops strategies to solve organizational problems. A novice or entry-level role was thought to be a communication technician who was focused on content generation and production of communication tactics. After further testing and analysis, these roles were compressed into two—manager or technician—and a practitioner could fulfill both but would be primarily one or the other (Travis and Lordan 2021; Dozier and Broom 1995).

The definition of the technician role is as before—one who produces tactics. They are known for proficiency in certain skills such as writing, graphic design, public speaking, use of social media and digital communications, or, more recently, being able to harness the power of big data and AI. Today, we call this individual a practitioner of public relations, taking the strategically planned campaign and creating campaign materials.

Meanwhile, the manager role is more complex. A manager thinks strategically and contributes to strategy development for the organization. A manager is part of the dominant coalition and, therefore, does not just communicate decisions but participates in making them. A manager does not just manage a public relations department but thinks in terms of managing the entire organization. Public relations from a management perspective is not done merely to gain attention and affect a nebulous image but is concerned with the development of mutually beneficial relationships that lead to a positive and stable reputation and the achievement of management goals consistent with an organization's mission (Dozier and Bloom 2006).

What is important theoretically and practically is that public relations professionals are not assigned a role—they must "enact" it. This means one could, and even should, act like a manager no matter what the job title or description. For some, acting like a manager will be obvious, such as someone hired as a chief communication officer with a seat automatically on the management team (i.e., "having a seat at the table"). But others may need to "manage up" by taking the initiative and offering suggestions that demonstrate a management mindset. In short, enactment means that a public relations professional consciously chooses a role and performs according to it. Having expertise is necessary but not sufficient to enact a manager role (Dozier and Bloom 2006). An entry-level employee may be prudent to wait to assume a manager role. But someone with the requisite knowledge and experience should not wait to be asked to step up.

The distinction of the two roles is more than just about individual career development. It affects the perception others have about the value of public relations as a profession, and it limits the benefit an organization could receive if professionals remain in a technician role. When public relations professionals say they desire "a seat at the table," they are expressing a desire to enact a manager role and bring the full perspective and benefit of public relations—positive relationships with multiple publics—to the leadership of the organization. It could be said that the manager role is true or professional public relations, whereas a technician role is evidence of a limited grasp of what public relations actually is: "We view organizational roles as central to our model of public relations practice and to our theory of the public relations function in organizations"

(Dozier and Broom 1995, 5). Meanwhile, professionals "who gravitate toward communication production activities—who define creativity largely in terms of the words and graphics they produce—find themselves at odds with the evolution of public relations into a true management-level profession" (Dozier and Broom 1995, 21).

Several factors have been determined that influence whether a professional decides to enact a manager role. Those more likely to do so are male, have a longer tenure with an employer, have an education in public relations and significant experience, and are part of a larger public relations staff. It should be noted, however, that sex and tenure are less of a predictor than earlier; for example, almost half of the CCOs who are members of the Arthur W. Page Society are female.

There are consequences to a professional not enacting a manager role. Professionals cannot perform at full capacity, with public relations reduced in that organization to a mere task and not a perspective. Also, the vacuum left on the management team will be filled by people from other organizational functions (see encroachment in next section).

In short, role enactment is about a public relations professional having a proper understanding of what public relations is and what it can do for organizations: "The value of public relations is not indicated by awards for tactics but the quality of mutually beneficial relationships that such communication helps establish with key publics" (Dozier and Broom 1995, 23).

The main way professionals can apply roles theory is with introspection about what they consider public relations to be, who they are as a professional, and how they can contribute fully to organizational success. Knowing the answer to those questions requires a deep understanding of public relations theory, and answering those questions with a manager mindset will result in the dual benefit of advancing an individual's career and enhancing organizational success.

Encroachment Theory

Even if professionals desire to enact a manager role, they may find barriers in the form of the dominant coalition sitting at the management table having a limited view of what public relations is. Or they could be stymied by encroachment, which means someone from another profession—marketing, human resources, law, finance—assumes the role of public relations. Sometimes, this happens because others see public relations as tactical message production or delivery only, so they take on message strategy and other aspects of a public relations manager's job, without professional public relations knowledge (i.e., theoretical foundation), to do so effectively and strategically.

As mentioned previously, assigning non-public relations functions to manage the public relations function is known as "encroachment" (Dozier 1988). The study of this phenomenon has shown that it takes three forms. One form exists when top management hires, promotes, or laterally moves individuals from some profession other than public relations to manage the public relations function. Like the penalty in football with the same name, it means someone crossed a line. Examples include hiring a public relations professional out of television journalism because they are seen as understanding the media, or promoting someone from marketing to manage a public relations department because they see public relations merely as media relations in support of marketing sales goals, or they ask a lawyer to serve as spokesperson to limit liability. This is unfortunately common, according to many professionals who have their copy edited or are compelled to communicate a decision or execute a strategy they deem professionally unwise or incomplete. But the consequence of encroachment is more than personal offense—it is a slight on the profession of public relations, which is relegated to little more than technical support (Lauzen 1992).

Another form exists when just as roles must be enacted, encroachment can be enabled or prevented by public relations professionals who refuse as much as organizational culture allows to prevent encroachment. If the top public relations professional in an organization aspires to a manager role, enacts a manager role, and has a powerful public relations "schema" (actually view public relations as a powerful organizational function), then the public relations function is likely to have more organizational power that will prevent encroachment (Lauzen 1992). Conversely, if the top public relations professional does not have the manager aspiration, enactment, and schema, they leave the door open for another function to take on what should be a public relations role.

Finally, seeing the need to obtain power and prevent encroachment also motivates some practitioners to seek more professional development:

> Theoretically, as the practitioner takes responsibility for the success or failure of public relations programs and makes communication policy decisions, the practitioner sees the need for formal education and training in public relations techniques and management. This powerful public relations schema then reinforces the practitioner's view that public relations requires strategic management (Lauzen 1992, 70).

Practically, there are four keys to building successful public relations departments that have organizational power and mitigate the risk of encroachment of the function. Professionals who are the top public relations person in their organization should take these items to heart as a professional challenge or share them with a colleague who is the senior practitioner:

1. The top public relations person aspires to a manager role;
2. The top public relations person has public relations competence (see next theory) to enact a manager role;
3. The top public relations person must believe and understand that public relations is a powerful organizational function, meaning it contributes across the enterprise and not just to managing itself as a function; and
4. The top public relations professional must behave consistently to enact the manager role (Lauzen 1992).

Public Relations Competence Theory

Any professional would like to think of themselves as competent. Competence is related to quality, professionalism, and effectiveness of practice. Stemming from the concepts of public relations technician and manager roles, as well as interpersonal communication competence, a *theory of public relations competence* was developed, incorporating aspects of a more general theory of communication competence (Habermas 1970), to explain why some people perform public relations roles better than others and make the transition from technician to manager role. The theory states that a competent public relations professional has a requisite level of public relations knowledge and skill and a motivation to enact a manager role. The context in which they work and the outcomes of public relations work are also considered (Hazelton 2006).

The theory was extended recently to look at the divergent views of public relations competence by professionals and the dominant coalition in their organizations (Knight and Sweetser 2021). The results showed that members of the dominant coalition saw a significant difference in the competence levels of public relations professionals who enacted a manager, as opposed to a technician role. They also saw more competence in a full-time public relations professional, as compared with some engaging in public relations activity part time or as a collateral duty. In another comparison, the dominant coalition rated the competence of public relations professionals lower than they rated themselves, but for those in a manager role, they rated the professionals higher than they rated themselves. Those who enacted a technician role can bring down the view organizational leaders have about the function of public relations overall. The context in which someone works explains why public relations professionals can be seen as competent by some but not by others or in one situation but not in another. For example, expectations for a public relations person to act as a manager versus a technician may be different in the military, corporation, nonprofit, as well as in sports or investor relations and other specific practice areas.

Public relations professionals can be motivated by this to seek competence for themselves. There are several ways to do this. If one does not have a formal degree in public relations, they could seek a master's degree to gain more formal education in the field. Seeking nondegree credentials such as certificates or accreditation in public relations (APR) from trade organizations can also bolster a professional's knowledge and perspective about the function of public relations. Consistent with role enactment, a professional can, over time, gain more advanced experience by enacting a manager role once they have more complete knowledge of the profession. Adopting a view of public relations as a management function and measuring success in terms of meeting organizational—not just communication—objectives will also contribute to a professional's competence in terms of both their self-perception and that of the leadership in their organization.

CHAPTER 17

Theories of Relationship and Engagement

Several of the theories mentioned previously emphasized that relationships should be at the core of public relations theory and practice. This case was made in 1984 by a graduate student, Mary Ann Ferguson, in a conference paper she presented (Ferguson 1984). Over the years, she received so many requests for that paper that in time the *Journal of Public Relations Research* decided to publish it. In 2018, it was the journal's most downloaded paper (Ferguson 2018).

Ferguson noted that from 1975 to 1984, another journal, *Public Relations Review*, had published few articles about theory—only 4 percent, with 54 percent being about practice and 44 percent introspective. She made the point then that in a field still maturing as an academic discipline, scholars needed to agree on a paradigm—a way of viewing what public relations is—before theory specific to the field could be developed. The practice was varied, and theory was lacking (Ferguson 2018).

A common understanding that public relations is about relationships would help advance public relations theory and inform the practice. It would focus on relationships rather than isolating organizations or publics and would therefore lead to a better understanding of what is important in those relationships to both organizations and their publics. At a macro level, a relationship focus could lend itself both to the development of public relations' own niche theory as well as be a lens through which to interpret findings from other fields. Research on relationships could be as broad or as narrow as the researcher would desire. Most importantly, relationship-focused research and theory, and from that practice, "will legitimize and define the field of public relations better than past efforts" (Ferguson 2018, 172).

A general focus on relationships soon became specified as organization–public relationships (OPRs). This came about because, even with a focus on relationships as the essence of public relations, the field had not settled on a definition. There were perspectives on relationships from interpersonal communications, psychotherapy, interorganizational relationships, and systems theory. But organization–public relations is a specific context and phenomenon and applied specifically to public relations as a profession (Broom et al. 1997).

The characteristics of relationships in an OPR context were theorized to include exchanges, transactions, communications, and other interconnected activities. Importantly, OPRs were seen to have antecedents and consequences that could guide further research and theory as well as inform practice (Heath 2013). The antecedents to OPRs include social and cultural norms, collective perspectives and expectations for the relationship, perceptions of an uncertain environment, a need for resources, and the degree to which a relationship is pursued for legal or voluntary reasons. The consequences of OPRs are goal achievement, dependency and loss of autonomy, and routine or institutionalized behavior (Broom et al. 1997).

Practically, relationships are seen as "patterns of linkages through which parties in the relationship pursue and service their interdependent needs" and, therefore, "relationship formation and maintenance represents a process of mutual adaptation and contingent responses" (Broom et al. 1997, 95). As for OPRs, specifically, only their characteristics were initially determined, although they had significant implications for practice. Professionals who consider why they and their publics want a relationship and how they enter into it, as well as the potential results of those relationships, will necessarily adapt communication strategy accordingly. In time, an actual definition of OPRs was offered that provides additional insight for public relations practice: "A state which exists between an organization and its key publics in which the outcomes of either entity impact the economic, social, political, and/or cultural well-being of the other entity" (Bruning and Ledingham 1999, 160). OPRs were also determined to have three dimensions: personal, professional, and community.

Typologies of OPRs were extended in the context of social media, although the results could be potentially applied to relationships offline as well. Relationship characteristics have been categorized as *strong*, seen in the intensity of interactions; *cohesive*, in which parties familiarize themselves or have an attraction toward a group; or *symmetrical*, which results from structures that enable two-way communication. Types of OPRs that result from relational characteristics are *exchange* (each party gives a benefit in the expectation of receiving a benefit), *communal* (one party gives a benefit in response to a need, without expectation of exchange), or *symbiotic* (both parties work together toward a common goal). Research revealed that strong relationship characteristics result in communal OPRs, cohesive relationship characteristics lead to communal and symbiotic OPRs, and symmetric relational characteristics result in exchange OPRs. In addition, both communal and exchange OPRs can foster symbiotic OPRs as well, or relationships of two types (Namisango and Kang 2019).

With a focus on relationships and particularly OPRs in the practice and theory of public relations, there was a felt need to standardize the measurement of OPRs. One effort employed an extensive survey with more than 30 items (Bruning and Ledingham 1999). A later measurement scale was refined to four items to measure the quality of OPRs. These included the degree of trust (confidence and willingness of one party to open up to another), satisfaction (the extent that one party feels favorably toward another because expectations for the relationship are met and reinforced), commitment (the relationship is seen as worth the energy to maintain and promote), and control mutuality (the parties agree who has the rightful power to influence the other) (Hon and Grunig 1999).

This OPR measurement scale was later extended for an international and multicultural context. The four items were seen as useful but also tied to Western culture. A fifth measure reflective of Eastern culture was added. *Renqing* and *mianzi*, or face and favor, are typical of Chinese culture in a relationship context. Face is related to putting forth a desirable image of self via social interactions, whereas favor involves leveraging a relationship with someone known in order to seek influence with someone less known. The concepts can be seen as "a strategy to be used or a resource to be exchanged" (Huang 2001, 69). Face and favor together were found to be a valid dimension for measuring OPRs in a multicultural context when conceived as a resource for exchange.

The theoretical concepts of relationships and OPRs serve as a foundation for this final section. The theories covered in this section are about relationships in various ways. First, several theories about conflict resolution and crisis communication are presented, since these concepts are vital to the maintenance of relationships. Second, a look at relationship management theory adds specificity to the concept of relationships from a theoretical perspective. A look at engagement theory is presented given the flourishing of that term in both theory and practice in an era of digital media, in particular. An explanation of co-creational theory reveals a perspective that organizational–public relationships are also a potential partnership. Finally, intercultural theory is revisited with a focus on relationship building and maintenance across cultures.

Crisis Communication Theories

Anyone who has a personal relationship knows they sometimes experience conflict. This is also true at the organization level. Sometimes, those conflictual situations are serious enough to be considered crises. From a public relations perspective, a *crisis* can be considered any relational conflict that has damaged or has the potential to damage an organization's reputation and/or operations. Because of this obvious threat, risk and crisis communications theories have emerged. This section looks at the most common ones.

The *contingency theory of strategic conflict management* (or *contingency theory*) began in the 1990s as a public relations theory and was based on a stance or position an organization takes in a conflict situation. That stance is contingent on internal and external variables. Internal variables are the characteristics of public relations professionals, the public relations department, the organization, the dominant coalition, internal threats, and relationship characteristics. In other words, attitudes about what public relations is and the duty to relationships affect a response to conflict. External variables include threats, the industry environment, all external publics, and political and social culture (Pang and Jin 2024).

The stances an organization takes exist on a continuum ranging from accommodation of public interest to advocacy for organizational interest. Many other potential stances exist between those two extremes. An examination of research studies identified 87 potential factors that influence an organization's stance at any given time toward a given public. As such, contingency theory of strategic conflict management sees public relations and its relationships as more complex and dynamic and cannot be simplified into models (Cameron et al. 2001, 2008; Cancel et al. 1999). Contingency theory of strategic conflict management also presupposes conflict in relationships and considers the essence of public relations to be managing those conflicts.

Another theory relative to relationship conflict and crisis is *image restoration theory*. The theory draws from a rhetorical perspective and is reactive in the sense that it considers a situation in which an offense has happened, and the organization is responsible (Benoit and Pang 2008). Image repair theory focuses on message content and determines a typology of five strategies to repair an organization's image after it has been damaged. The theory does not necessarily claim these strategies are persuasive and effective but only that they are the observed nature of responses given by organizations:

- Denial—deny responsibility or shift blame to others;
- Evade Responsibility—this includes statements such as the organization was provoked, did not have adequate information, the offensive occurrence was an accident, or the organization acted with good intentions;
- Reduce Offensiveness—there are multiple strategies within this message category: bolstering (stress the organization's good traits), minimizing (claim the offense was not as bad as it is being made to seem); differentiation (the offense in question was less offensive than other acts by others); transcendence (there are more important things to consider); attack the accuser (reduce the credibility of the accuser, commonly called "gaslighting"); compensation (reimburse those offended in some way);
- Corrective Action—announce a plan (and enact it) to prevent similar problems in the future;
- Mortification—apology. This must be genuine and shown, not merely stated (Benoit 1995).

The strategy employed should be appropriate to the situation, especially the degree to which an organization is at fault and the severity of the offense. Truth should be the guide for practitioners planning an organizational response. An additional guiding perspective for professionals may sound semantic, but it is critical. Even though the theory employs the word "image," a good strategic consideration would be to use the term "reputation" instead. An image connotes something abstract and fleeting and can be created with words and is thus ripe for manipulation. A reputation is concrete and based on the experience of people; it is formed in their own minds, and an organization earns a reputation. Focusing on image can lead to dishonest messages to try to force a positive perspective in publics in the short term. A reputation is a long-term view, controlled by the public, and professionals who recognize this are more likely to be honest, transparent, and authentic in communications, which is more likely to be effective in generating a positive perception of the organization by its publics.

The most-often cited theory about crisis communications is Coombs' *situational crisis communication theory* (SCCT). The theory is based on attribution theory (explained in Chapter 10). Essentially, attribution theory says persuasion is dependent not just on messages but on what the public attributes an organization's intentions to in communicating. In the context of responding to a crisis, the public's opinion about a crisis response message is affected by their attribution of responsibility for the crisis. There are a myriad of types of crises that have happened and that could happen, but SCCT is helpful in that it organizes types of crises into three categories, called clusters, based on attribution of responsibility. The clusters are *preventable*, which implies mismanagement and a high level of organizational responsibility; *accident*, which means the organization had a moderate degree of responsibility and perhaps did not have bad intent; and the *victim* cluster, in which there is weak to no responsibility associated by the public (Coombs 2006). Preventable crises could be recalls of products, investors deceived, misconduct, or ethical violations. Crises resulting from accidents could be damage caused, equipment failure, or weak oversight of operations. The victim type of crises could be natural disasters, workplace violence, rumors, and product tampering.

The real value for practice of SCCT is the association of specific strategies of crisis response for each crisis cluster. The strategies are similar to those in previous theories but are arranged according to three postures or attitudes an organization might take with regard to the publics in a specific crisis:

- Deny posture (best used with victim cluster crises):
  - Attack the accuser;
  - Deny the crisis happened, its severity, or organizational responsibility; and
  - Scapegoat, blame others for the crisis.
- Diminish posture (best used with accident cluster crises):
  - Excuse, deny the intent to do harm, or claim an inability to control the situation; and
  - Justification, minimize perceived damage, and say the organization had to act the way it did;
- Deal posture (best used with preventable cluster crises):
  - Ingratiation, remind public of past good deeds by the organization;
  - Concern, show compassion toward publics affected by crisis;
  - Compensation, pay for damage, offer discount or other financial or other forms of repayment;
  - Regret, statement that the organization feels bad for the publics' harm; and
  - Apology, a full ownership of responsibility (Coombs 1995, 2008).

While effective response to a crisis has obvious implications for organizational reputation, SCCT stresses that reputation management should come *after* addressing public interest. Public interest messaging includes instructing information, or telling people how to protect themselves in a crisis, and adjusting information, assisting publics in coping emotionally and psychologically after a crisis. This public interest messaging will do more to build and maintain a positive reputation. It is also notable that a positive prior reputation can aid with public opinion when a crisis does occur. People are less likely to attribute responsibility to an organization that has maintained a good reputation (Coombs 2007).

In addition to maintaining a positive reputation and practicing ethically, crises can be prevented through application of *issues management theory* (Jones and Chase 1979; Coombs et al. 2019). Issues are conceived as brewing crises not yet risen to full public or media attention. Responding to issues before they are crises is therefore a proactive crisis strategy. Managing issues follows a five-step model:

1. Identify issues through environmental scanning.
2. Prioritize issues according to relevance to the organization (likely to escalate and severity of potential harm).
3. Select a response strategy (could be from other theories, dependent on public and situation).
4. Create and implement a response.
5. Evaluate the effort to see if the issue is resolved or requires more response (Jones and Chase 1979).

This body of theories is extensive but strategically helpful to practitioners. Crises should not all be seen the same way or only as a threat to the organization. Instead, they should be viewed through the lens of organizational responsibility. Often, publics are not angry but seeking information that an organization can provide, especially with modern communication tools such as social media (Jin and Spence 2023). Crisis communication can then be more strategic by matching messages to the type of crisis and public attitude. Measurement of the success of crisis communication should not focus on public attention simmering down but the ongoing positive reputation and relationship with affected publics.

Relationship Management Theory

The emphasis on relationships as central to public relations led to the proposal of a specific *relationship management theory*. This theory also responds to public relations being conceived as a management function; the emphasis on measuring how OPRs affect public attitudes, perceptions, knowledge, and behavior; and theoretical models that accommodate relationship antecedents and consequences (Ledingham 2006).

Relationship management theory therefore takes the perspective that public relations balances the interests of organizations and publics through the management of organization–public relationships. The theory is consistent with the definition of public relations as "the management function that establishes and maintains mutually beneficial relationships between an organization and publics on whom its success or failure depends" (Cutlip et al. 1994, 2). The theory exemplifies the definition of the profession, and, therefore, management of relationships is "the appropriate framework for the study, teaching and practice of public relations" (Ledingham 2003, 195).

Based on an extensive review of other theories and research literature in public relations, relationship management theory offers a summative proposition: "Effectively managing organizational–public relationships around common interests and shared goals, over time, results in mutual understanding and benefit for interacting organizations and publics" (Ledingham 2003, 190).

The theory is considered a "general" theory in that it provides unifying concepts, many of which are drawn from other established theories. The basic concepts of relationship management theory are as follows:

- The appropriate domain of public relations is that of relationships.
- Organizational–public relationships (OPRs) are transactional and dynamic.
- OPRs are goal oriented.
- OPRs have antecedents and consequences.
- OPRs are driven by perceived needs and wants of organizations and publics.
- The continuation of relationships depends on needs being met.
- Communication is not the sole instrument of relationship building.
- Types of OPRs are personal, professional, and community.
- OPRs can be seen as symbolic or behavioral.
- The effective management of relationships results in mutual benefit (Ledingham 2006).

These concepts may seem like a lot for a professional to take in and apply. But collectively, the theory's concepts should lead to a single strategic framework for organizations building relationships with publics. Professionals should see the work of public relations as being focused on relationships, then understand how and why publics want relationships with an organization (not only the other way around). Well-managed relationships yield countless benefits, such as membership retention (Pressgrove et al. 2024). And, finally, work to apply the principles to maintain those relationships and achieve mutual benefit.

Engagement Theory

Engagement is another term that is routinely used by professionals and scholars discussing public relations practice. The use of engagement theory is especially the case in the context of digital communications, which facilitates and is measured by engagement. The term first appeared as a theoretical concept in the 1990s, and research on the subject peaked in 2014 (Jelen-Sanchez 2017). However, engagement has rarely been clearly defined and is often used as a synonym for dialogue, interaction, or participation. Many professionals see engagement as something they need to quantify to prove success. It has been seen as a phenomenon that organizations need to manage for their benefit rather than understand in terms of the dynamics of interactions with publics (Jelen-Sanchez 2017).

The concept of engagement has been formally studied in five communication contexts: social media, employee engagement, CSR and engagement, civic engagement and social capital, and dialogic engagement for ethical practice. In spite of the research attention, the public relations profession needs to further develop the concept (Jelen-Sanchez 2017).

One description of engagement that gives it such distinction from other terms has been offered: "Engagement involves publics in agenda setting, decision making and policy formation and as such extends beyond dialogue" (Jelen-Sanchez 2017, 7).

Just as in interpersonal relationships, where an engagement is more significant than dating, in OPRs engagement means more than dialogue. It certainly means more than garnering clicks, likes, shares, and comments. It has more to do with participation than response. Professionals would do well to consider the full meaning of engagement and in so doing, will make it more meaningful to publics and therefore beneficial to the organization.

Co-creational Theory

Similar to the notion in engagement theory that organizations work in partnership with publics, *co-creational theory* positions organizations on an equal footing with multiple publics. There are several propositions in the theory:

- Organizations do not cede power but share in the creation of issues with multiple publics.
- Organizations do not resist change but embrace it as a component of relationships.
- Public relations professionals view the communication process as two-way and dynamic.
- Public relations professionals do not view the organization as the hub or center but as a spoke in the wheel (Travis and Lordan 2021).

Co-creational theory would be evident in forms of communication such as encouraging user-generated content, inviting representatives of various publics to be on advisory committees; convening meetings or even sponsoring community initiatives to address issues; or allowing, inviting, and responding to input on websites and social channels. Public relations professionals can apply these principles by intentionally and strategically incorporating co-creation opportunities into campaigns or ongoing corporate communications. This has benefits, including enhancing the strength of OPRs, ensuring the appropriateness and originality of content, fending off potential crises, demonstrating a CSR or CSA mindset of the organization, and meeting organizational objectives, including a positive reputation.

Theory of Intercultural Public Relations

Intercultural theories were earlier covered with regard to understanding audiences. Here, the focus is on the relational aspect of public relations, specifically in intercultural settings. The *theory of intercultural public relations* addresses reconsidering the segmentation of publics. Often, this is done by demographics—age, gender, race—or the way an organization categorizes stakeholders, such as employees, customers, donors, investors, and community. This theory suggests consideration of cultural identity, which is broader and deeper than race (Sha 2006). Nevertheless, the bulk of academic literature does not address cultural identity with regard to the behavior and relationships of organizations and their publics.

A study to consider this way of segmenting publics found that non-White publics were more likely to recognize racio-ethnic problems, feel personally involved with these problems, and engage in communication behavior about these problems (Sha 2006). STOPS, mentioned previously, is relevant in that publics can be segmented according to problems. Professionals could also consider communicating in culturally sensitive ways to be both more effective and ethical.

Intercultural public relations according to this theory is defined as "as [a] special case of public relations in which the salient cultural identity avowed by the organization differs from the salient cultural identity avowed by the public" (Sha 2006, 54). The theory therefore predicts that in situations where a cultural identity is salient, differences in cultural identity between an organization and a public will result in differences for that public in problem recognition, level of involvement, constraint recognition, and type of communication behavior—a specified application of the variables in STOPS.

Therefore, "if an organization and its publics hold different avowed identities salient to the situation, intercultural public relations becomes a necessary aspect of excellent public relations" (Sha 2006, 46). The application makes sense for NGOs and MNCs, but even domestically in environments where a variety of cultural identities exist, organizations need to be ever vigilant in practicing intercultural public relations. This means listening to unique perspectives and being open to learning about unforeseen needs or problems. It also requires not defining "intercultural" as only about race or ethnicity. Each nation has multiple ethnic groups, which in turn have many cultural identities. Other demographic categories can also be considered cultural identities, such as religion, age, or ideology. Taking a broader lens to segmenting publics will yield more specific and positive results for organizations' ongoing relationships with multiple publics.

Strategic Summary of Part VI—Public Relations Management

Theories specifically about public relations enable professionals to have a thorough understanding of the essence of the profession. Strategic insights from these theories not only help guide practice but should also elevate practice to the level where it is seen as a vital management function by clients and the C-Suite of organizations.

- Good standards for public relations practice involve following a process that includes research, setting objectives, determining strategy, choosing appropriate tactics, and measuring whether objectives were met.
- Objectives should be about *outcome* (how the publics respond in terms of changes in awareness, attitude, and action) and not merely *output*, which is what the public relations professional produces and distributes.
- Public relations objectives should align with fulfilling management objectives.
- The top public relations professional in an organization should report directly to the CEO and not to any other function.
- Publics engage with organizations because they have a problem to solve and not just to respond to communication from the organization. Their level of attention and type of response to public relations communication are based on the degree of their motivation to solve a problem.
- There are essentially two roles in public relations—technician or manager—and professionals need to "enact" a manager role instead of waiting to be consulted or promoted.
- Failure to enact a manager role means the function of public relations in an organization will be diminished in the perception of organizational leadership or the dominant coalition.
- When the public relations professional does not enact a manager role and provide insight into organizational decision

making with regard to public relationships, the function of public relations will be encroached on or assumed by people in other professions and functions.

- A public relations professional is said to be competent if they have a level of knowledge, experience, and a desire to enact a manager role in the organization.
- Public relations is about a unique form of relationship called an OPR—organization–public relationship—in which each impacts the well-being of the other.
- Relationships or OPRs can and should be measured according to trust, satisfaction, commitment, and control mutuality as a key indicator of public relations success.
- Crisis communication should be approached by first determining the type of crisis based on the level of organizational responsibility and then determining the appropriate response strategy or strategies.
- Public relations professionals should consider how an individual or public's cultural identity will affect how they receive, understand, and respond to public relations efforts.

References

Abrams, D., M. A. Hogg, S. Hinkle, and S. Otten. 2005. "The Social Identity Perspective on Small Groups." In *Theories of Small Groups: Interdisciplinary Perspectives*, edited by M. S. Poole and A. B. Hollingshead. Sage.

Akim, Feride. 2018. "The Education of Public Relations Students on Public Relations Theories: An Investigation on the Curriculum of Public Relations Departments of Communication Faculties in Turkey." *Intermedia International e-Journal* 5 (9).

Alfano, M. R., J. A. Carter, and M. Cheong. 2018. Technological Seduction and Self-Radicalization. *Journal of the American Philosophical Association* 4 (3): 298–322.

Arnstein, S. 1969. "A Ladder of Citizen Participation." *Institute of Planners Journal* 35 (4): 216–224.

Arthur W. Page Center. 2024. *Ethical Decision-Making Models.* November 19. https://archive.pagecentertraining.psu.edu/public-relations-ethics/lesson-2/ethical-decision-making-models.

Ashforth, B., and F. Mael. 1989. "Social Identity Theory and the Organization." *Academy of Management Review* 14 (1): 20–39.

Azjen, I. 1991. "The Theory of Planned Behavior." *Organizational Behavior and Human Decision Processes* 50: 179–211.

Baker, S., and D. L. Mortinson. 2001. "The TARES Test: Five Principles for Ethical Persuasion." *Journal of Mass Media Persuasion* 16 (2 & 3): 148–175.

Ball-Rokeach, Sandra, J., and Melvin L. DeFleur. 1976. "A Dependency Model of Mass-Media Effects." *Communication Research* 3: 3–21.

Bandura, A. 1977. *Social Learning Theory.* Prentice Hall.

Bang, T. 2019. "Ethics." In *Public Relations Theory: Application and Understanding*, edited by Brigitta Brunner. John Wiley and Sons.

Basareba, N., P. Arnds, J. Edmond, and O. Conlon. 2021. "New Media Ecology and Theoretical Foundations for Nonfiction Digital Narrative Creative Practice." *Narrative* 29 (3): 374–395.

Benoit, W. L. 1995. *Accounts, Excuses and Apologies: A Theory of Image Restoration.* State University of New York.

Benoit, William L., and Augustine Pang. 2008. "Crisis Communication and Image Repair Discourse." In *Public Relations: From Theory to Practice*, edited by T. Hanson-Horn and Bonita Neff. Allyn and Bacon.

Berger, C. R., and R. J. Calabrese. 1975. "Some Explanations in Initial Interactions and Beyond: Towards a Developmental Theory of Interpersonal Communication." *Human Communication Research* 1: 99–112.

Bormann, E. G. 1982. "The Symbolic Convergence Theory of Communication: Applications and Implications for Teachers and Consultants." *Journal of Applied Communication Research* 10: 50–61.

Bowen, S. 2005. "A Practical Model for Ethical Decision-Making in Issues Management and Public Relations." *Journal of Public Relations Research* 17 (3): 191–216.

Bowen, S. 2008. "Foundations in Moral Philosophy for Public Relations Ethics." In *Public Relations: From Theory to Practice*, edited by T. Hanson-Horn and B. Neff. Allyn and Bacon.

Bowman, S., and J. Hendy. 2019. "A Liquid Profession: An Ecological Approach to the Theory and Knowledge That Underpin the Practice of Public Relations." *Public Relations Inquiry* 8 (3): 333–351.

Brehmer, B. 1988. "The Development of Social Judgment Theory." In *Human Judgment: The SJT View*, edited by B. Brehmer and C. R. Joyce. Elsevier.

Broom, G. M., S. Casey, and J. Ritchey. 1997. "Toward a Concept and Theory of Organization-Public Relationships." *Journal of Public Relations Research* 9 (2): 83–98.

Bruning, S. D., and J. A. Ledingham. 1999. "Relationships between Organizations and Publics: Development of a Multi-Dimensional Organization-Public Relationship Scale." *Public Relations Review* 25 (2): 157–170.

Brunner, Brigitta R. 2019. *Public Relations Theory: Application and Understanding.* Wiley.

Buber, M. 1958. *I and Thou.* Translated by R. G. Smith. T&T Clark.

Burgoon, Judee K. 1993. "Interpersonal Expectations, Expectancy Violations and Emotional Communication." *Journal of Language and Social Psychology* 12 (1): 30–48.

Burgoon, J. K., and A. S. Hubbard. 2005. "Cross-Cultural and Intercultural Applications of Expetancy Violation Theory and Interaction Adaptation Theory." In *Theorizing About Intercultural Communication*, edited by W. B. Gudykunst. Sage.

Burgoon, M., and L. B. King. 1974. The Mediation of Resistance to Persuasion Strategies by Language Variables and Active-Passive Participation. *Human Communication Research* 1 (1): 30–41.

Burleson, B. R., and S. L. Kline. 1979. "Habermas' Theory of Communication: A Critical Explication." *Quarterly Journal of Speech* 65: 412–428.

Butcher, J. 2023. *DEI Has Failed and We Do Not Need More of It.* The Heritage Foundation. https://www.heritage.org/education/commentary/dei-has-failed -we-do-not-need-more-it

Cameron, G. T., F. Crupp, and B. H. Reber. 2001. "Getting Past Platitudes: Factors Limiting Accommodation in Public Relations." *Journal of Communication Management* 5 (3): 242–261.

Cameron, Glen, Augustine Pang, and Yan Jin. 2008. "Contingency Theory: Strategic Management of Conflict in Public Relations." In *Public Relations: From Theory to Practice*, edited by T. Hanson-Horn and B. Neff. Allyn and Bacon.

Cancel, A. E., M. A. Mitrook, and G. T. Cameron. 1999. "Testing the Contingency Theory of Accommodation in Public Relations." *Public Relations Review* 25 (2): 171–197.

Carden, A. R. 2008. "Working with Innovators and Laggards:." In *Public Relations: From Theory to Practice*, edited by T. Hansen-Horn and B. Neff. Pearson.

Carey, J. W. 1975. "A Cultural Approach to Communication." *Communication* 2: 11–22.

Carr, Caleb T. 2021. *Computer-Mediated Communication: A Theoretical and Practical Introduction to Online Human Communication*. Rowman & Littlefield.

Chen, Yi-Ru Regina, Chun-Ju Flora Hung-Baesecke, and Xianhong Chen. 2020. "Moving Forward the Dialogic Theory of Public Relations: Concepts, Methods and Applications of Organization-Public Dialogue." *Public Relations Review* 46 (1): 1–6.

Cialdini, R. B. 1993. *Influence: Science and Practice*. Harper Collins.

Cialdini, R. B. 1994. "Interpersonal Influence." In *Persuasion: Psychological Insights and Perspectives*, edited by T. Shavitt and T. Brook. Allyn and Bacon.

Claeys, A., and M. Opgenhoffen. 2016. "Why Practitioners Do (Not) Apply Crisis Communication Theory in Practice." *Journal of Public Relations Research* 28 (5–6): 232–247.

Collier, M. J., and M. Thomas. 1988. "Cultural Identity: An Interpretive Perspective." In *Theories in Intercultural Communication*, edited by Y. Y. Kim and W. B. Gudykunst. Sage.

Commission on Education in Public Relations. 2023. "Navigating Change: Recommendations for Advancing Undergraduate Public Relations Education." *Commission on Public Relations Education*. https://www.commissionpred.org/navigating-change-report/.

Compton, Josh, Shelley Wigley, and Sergei A. Samoilenko. 2021. "Inoculation Theory and Public Relations." *Public Relations Review* 47 (5): 1–6.

Coombs, W. T. 1995. "Choosing the Right Words: The Development of Guidelines for the Selection of the 'Appropriate' Crisis Response Strategies." *Management Communication Quarterly* 8: 447–476.

Coombs, W. T. 2006. "Crisis Management: A Communication Approach." In *Public Relations Theory II*, edited by C. Botan and V. Hazleton. Lawrence Erlbaum Associates.

Coombs, W. T. 2007. "Protecting Organizational Reputations During a Crisis: The Development and Application of the Situational Crisis Communication Theory." *Corporate Reputation Review* 10: 163–176.

Coombs, W. T. 2008. "The Development of the Situational Crisis Communication Theory." In *Public Relations: From Theory to Practice*, edited by T. Hanson-Horn and B. Neff. Allyn and Bacon.

Coombs, W. T., S. J. Halladay, and E. Tachkova. 2019. "Crisis Communication, Risk Communication, and Issues Management." In *Public Relations Theory: Application and Understanding*, edited by B. Brunner. Wiley.

Cooney, J. 2017. "Reflections on the 27th Anniversary of the Term 'Social License'." *Journal of Energy and Natural Resources Law* 35 (2): 197–200.

Crowley, A. E., and W. D. Hoyer. 1994. "An Integrative Framework for Understanding Two-Sided Persuasion." *Journal of Consumer Research* 20 (4): 561–574.

Cutlip, S. M., A. H. Center, and G. H. Broom. 1994. *Effective Public Relations*. Prentice Hall.

Dainton, Marianne, and Elaine D. Zelley. 2023. *Applying Communication Theory for Professional Life: A Practical Introduction*. Sage.

Dam, Linda, A. M. Barsoi Basaram, and David Atkin. 2021. "Fear of COVID-19 Opinion Expression: Digitally Mediated Spirals of Silence and the Situational Theory of Problem Solving." *Journal of Broadcasting and Electronic Media* 65 (4): 457–478.

Davidson, Scott. 2020. "Made by a Human Like You or Me: Back to the Greek Classics to Further Develop the Rhetorical Paradigm of Public Relations." *Public Relations Review* 46 (1): 1–6.

Dewey, John. 1910. *How We Think*. Heath.

Dietrich, Gini. 2024. "What is the PESO Model?" *SPINSUCKS*. https://spinsucks.com/communication/peso-model-breakdown/.

Dillard, J. P., and D. H. Salomon. 2005. "Measuring the Realms of Relational Frames: A Relational Framing Theory Perspective." In *The Sourcebook of Nonverbal Measures: Going Beyond Words*, edited by V. Mansau. Lawrence Erlbaum Associates.

Dillingham, L. L., and B. Ivanov. 2017. "Inoculation Messages as Preemptive Financial Crisis Communication Strategy for Inexperienced Investors." *Journal of Applied Communication Research* 45 (3): 274–293.

Dozier, D. M. 1988. "Breaking Public Relations' Glass Ceiling." *Public Relations Review* 14: 6–13.

Dozier, D. M., and G. Bloom. 2006. "The Centrality of Practitioner Roles to Public Relations Theory." In *Public Relations Theory II*, edited by C. Botan and V. Hazleton. Lawrence Erlbaum Associates.

Dozier, D. M., and G. M. Broom. 1995. "Evolution of the Manager Role in Public Relations Practice." *Journal of Public Relations Research* 7 (1): 3–26.

Dzage, E. J., and A. Pierog. 2023. "Corporate Social Responsibility and Sustainability in the Context of Change: Influence of the Stakeholder Theory." *SEA—Political Application of Science* 33 (3): 153–164.

Easley, R. W., W. O. Bearden, and J. E. Teel. 1995. "Testing Predictions Derived from Inoculation Theory and the Effectiveness of Self-Disclosure Communication Strategies." *Journal of Business Research* 34: 93–105.

Emerson, R. M. 1962. "Power-Dependence Relations." *American Sociological Review* 27: 31–41.

Fairhurst, G., and R. Sarr. 1996. *The Art of Framing.* Jossey-Bass.

Ferguson, M. A. 1984. "Building Theory in Public Relations: Interorganizational Relationships." *Association of Education in Journalism and Mass Communication.*

Ferguson, Mary Ann. 2018. "Building Theory in Public Relations: Interorganizational Relationships as a Public Relations Paradigm." *Journal of Public Relations Research* 30 (4): 164–178.

Festinger, L. 1957. *A Theory of Cognitive Dissonance.* Stanford University Press.

Fishbein, M., and I. Ajzen. 1975. *Belief, Attitude, Intention and Behavior: An Introduction to Theory and Research.* Addison-Wesley.

Fitzpatrick, Kathy. n.d. "Ethical Decision-Making Guide Helps Resolve Ethical Issues." Accessed November 20, 2024. https://www.prsa.org/docs/default-source/about/ethics/ethics-case-studies/ethics-case-study-ethical-decision-making-guide.pdf?sfvrsn=8a55268f_4.

Freeman, R. E. 1984. *Strategic Management: A Stakeholder Approach.* Pitron.

Gaara, A., M. Kaptein, and G. Berens. 2024. "It Is All in the Name: Toward a Typology of Public Relations Professionals' Ethical Dilemmas." *Public Relations Review* 50 (1).

Gearhardt, S., and W. Zhang. 2018. "Same Spiral, Different Day? Testing the Spiral of Silence Across Issue Types." *Communication Research* 45 (1): 34–54.

Gerbner, G., L. Gross, M. Morgan, and N. Signorelli. 1980. "The Mainstreaming of America: Violence Profile No. 11." *Journal of Communication* 30: 10–29.

Gerbner, George, Larry Gross, Michael Morgan, and Nancy Signorelli. 1986. "Living with Television: The Dynamics of the Cultivation Process." In *Perspectives on Media Effects*, edited by Jennings Bryant and Dolf Zillman. Lawrence Erlbaum Associates.

Ghanem, S. 1997. "Filling in the Tapestry: The Second-Level of Agenda Setting." In *Communication and Democracy: Exploring the Intellectual Frontiers of Agenda Setting Theory*, edited by M. McCombs, D. L. Shaw, and D. Weaver. Routledge.

Giddens, Anthony. 1984. *The Constitution of Society: Outline of the Theory of Structuration.* Oxford University Press.

Global Alliance. 2012. *The Melbourne Mandate.* https://www.globalalliancepr.org/melbourne-mandate.

Goffman, E. 1974. *Frame Analysis: An Essay on the Organization of Experience.* Harper and Row.

Gower, K. 2003. *Legal and Ethical Constraints on Public Relations.* Waveland Press.

Graham, J., J. Haidt, S. Koleva, et al. 2013. "Moral Foundations Theory: The Pragmatic Validity of Moral Pluralism." *Advances in Experimental Social Psychology* 47: 55–130.

Grunig, James. 1989. "Symmetrical Presuppositions as a Framework for Public Relations Theory." In *Public Relations Theory*, edited by C. Botan and V. Hazleton. Lawrence Erlbaum Associates.

Grunig, James E., ed. 1992. *Excellence in Public Relations and Communication Management.* Lawrence Erlbaum Associates.

Grunig, J. E., and L. A. Grunig. 2006. "The Excellence Theory." In *Public Relations Theory II*, edited by C. Botan and V. Hazleton. Lawrence Erlbaum Associates.

Grunig, J. E., and F. C. Repper. 1992. "Strategic Management, Publics and Issues." In *Excellence in Communication and Public Relations Management*, edited by J. E. Grunig. Lawrence Erlbaum Associates.

Habermas, J. 1970. "Toward a Theory of Communication Competence." *Inquiry* 13 (4): 360–375.

Habermas, J. 1984. *The Theory of Communicative Action.* Translated by T. McCarthy. Beacon Press.

Habermas, J. 1991. *The Structural Transformation of the Public Sphere.* MIT Press.

Haigh, M. M., and S. Wigley. 2015. "Examining the Impact of Negative, User-Generated Content on Stakeholders." *Corporate Communications an International Journal* 20 (1): 63–75.

Hall, E. T. 1976. *Beyond Culture.* Archer.

Hamm, Joseph A., S. E. Wolfe, C. Cavanaugh, and Sung Lee. 2022. "Organizing Legitimacy Theory." *Legal and Criminological Psychology* 27 (2): 129–146.

Hayes, A. F. 2007. "Exploring the Forms of Self-Censorship: On the Spiral of Silence and the Use of Opinion Expression Avoidance Strategies." *Journal of Communication* 57 (4): 785–802.

Hayes, Rebecca A., Stephanie L. Robertson, and Allison N. Preston. 2023. "Does Public Relations Scholarship Need Better PR? Practitioners' Perspectives on Academic Research." *Public Relations Review* 49 (1): 1–7.

Hazelton, V. 2006. "Toward a Theory of Public Relations Competence." In *Public Relations Theory II*, edited by C. Botan and V. Hazleton, 199–222. Lawrence Erlbaum Associates.

Hazelton, V., and C. H. Botan. 1999. "The Role of Theory in Public Relations." In *Public Relations Theory*, edited by C. Botan and V. Hazleton. Lawrence Erlbaum Associates.

Heath, R. L. 2013. "The Journey to Understand and Champion OPR Takes Many Roads, Some Not Yet Well-Travelled." *Public Relations Review* 39: 426–431.

Heider, I. 1946. "Attitudes and Cognitive Organization." *Journal of Psychology* 21 (1): 107–112.

Herzog, H. 1944. "What Do We Really Know about Daytime Serial Listeners?" In *Radio Research*, edited by P. F. Lazersfeld and E. N. Stanton. Duell, Sloan and Pearce.

Ho, B., W. Shin, and A. Pang. 2016. "Corporate Crisis Advertising: A Framework Examining the Use and Effects of Corporate Advertising Before and After a Crisis." *Journal of Marketing Communication* 23 (7): 537–551.

Hobbs, Mitchell John, and Sarah O'Keefe. 2024. "Agonism in the Arena: Analyzing Cancel Culture Using a Rhetorical Model of Deviance and Reputational Repair." *Public Relations Review* 50 (1).

Hoewe, J., and D. R. Ewoldson. 2024. "The Media Use Model: A Metatheoretical Framework for Media Processes and Effects." *Human Communication Research* 50 (2): 254–263.

Hofstede, G. 1980. *Culture's Consequences: International Differences in Work-Related Roles*. Sage.

Hofstede, G., and G. J. Hofstede. 2005. *Cultures and Organizations: Software of the Mind*. Vol. 2. McGraw Hill.

Hollingshead, A. B., G. M. Wittenbaum, P. B. Paulus, et al. 2005. "A Look at Groups from the Functional Perspective." In *Theories of Small Groups: An Interdisciplinary Perspective*, edited by M. S. Poole and A. B. Hollingshead. Sage.

Holmes, P. E., and M. C. Hawood. 2023. "The Duplicitous Effect of Organizational Identification: Applying Social Identity Theory to Identify Joint Relations with Workplace Social Courage and Unethical Pro-Organizational Behavior." *Journal of Positive Psychology* 18 (5): 784–797.

Holtzhausen, D. 2015. "The Unethical Consequences of Professional Communication Codes of Ethics: A Postmodern Analysis of Ethical Decision-Making in Communication Practice." *Public Relations Review* 41 (5): 769–776.

Hon, L. C., and J. Grunig. 1999. "Guide to Measuring Relationships." *Institute for Public Relations*. http://www.instituteforpr.com/pdf/1999_guide_measure_relationships.pdf.

Huang, M., and E.-J. Ki. 2023. "Protecting Organizational Reputation during a Para Crisis: The Effectiveness of Conversational Human Voice on Social Media and the Roles of Construal Level, Social Presence, and Organizational Listening." *Public Relations Review* 49 (5).

Huang, Y. 2001. "OPRA: A Cross-Cultural Multi-Factor Scale for Measuring Organization-Public Relationships." *Journal of Public Relations Research* 13 (1): 61–90.

Hughes, C. 2024. The End of Race Politics: Arguments for a Colorblind America. Penguin.

International Public Relations Association. 2020. "Code of Conduct." https://www.ipra.org/member-services/code-of-conduct/.

Jagdeep, Ankita, Anisha Jagdeep, Simon Lazarus, et al. 2024. "Instructing Animosity: How DEI Pedagogy Produces The Hostile Attribution Bias." Rutgers University Social Perception Lab. https://networkcontagion.us/wp-content/uploads/Instructing-Animosity_11.13.24.pdf

Janis, Irving. 1982. *Victims of Groupthink: A Psychological Study of Foreign Decisions and Fiascos.* Houghton Mifflin.

Jelen-Sanchez, A. 2017. "Engagement in Public Relations Discipline: Themes, Theoretical Perspectives, and Methodological Approaches." *Public Relations Review* 43 (5): 934–944.

Jenkins, H., S. Ford, and J. Green. 2013. *Spreadable Media: Creating Value and Meaning in a Networked Culture.* New York University Press.

Jeong, S. 2009. "Public's Responses to an Oil Spill Accident: A Test of the Attribution Theory and Situational Crisis Communication Theory." *Public Relations Review* 35: 307–309.

Jin, X., and P. R. Spence. 2023. "Check Crisis Information on Twitter: Information Flow and Crisis Communication Patterns of Hurricane Ida." *Communication Studies* 74 (4): 337–355.

Jones, B. C., and W. H. Chase. 1979. "Managing Public Policy Issues." *Public Relations Review* 5 (2): 3–23.

Karzenny, F. 1978. "A Theory of Electronic Propinquity: Mediated Communication in Organizations." *Communication Research* 5: 3–24.

Katz, E., J. G. Blumler, and M. Gurevitch. 1973. "Uses and Gratifications Research." *Public Opinion Quarterly* 37: 509–523.

Katz, E., J. G. Blumler, and M. Gurevitch. 1974. "Uses of Mass Communication by the Individual." In *Mass Communication Research: Major Issues and Future Directions*, edited by W. P. Davison and F. T. Yu. Praeger.

Kelleher, T. 2009. "Conversational Voice, Communicated Committment, and Public Relations Outcomes in Interactive Online Communication." *Journal of Communication* 59: 172–188.

Kent, Michael, and Chaoyuan Li. 2020. "Toward a Normative Social Media Theory for Public Relations." *Public Relations Review* 46 (1): 1–10.

Kent, M. L., and M. Taylor. 1998. "Building Dialogic Relationships Through the World Wide Web." *Public Relations Review* 24: 273–288.

Kent, M. L., and M. Taylor. 2002. "Toward a Dialogic Theory of Public Relations." *Public Relations Review* 28: 21–37.

Kim, Jeong-Nam, and James E. Grunig. 2011. "Problem Solving and Communicative Action: A Situational Theory of Problem Solving." *Journal of Communication* 61: 120–149.

Kim, S. 2013. "Does Corporate Advertising Work in a Crisis? An Extension of Inoculation Theory." *Journal of Marketing Communication* 19 (4): 293–305.

Kim, Soo-Yeon, and Eyun-Jung Ki. 2014. "An Exploratory Study of Ethics Codes of Professional Public Relations Associations: Proposing Modified Universal Codes of Ethics in Public Relations." *Journal of Mass Media Ethics* 29 (4): 238–257.

Kim, Y. Y. 2001. *Becoming Intercultural: An Integrative Theory of Communication and Cross-Cultural Adaptation.* Sage.

Kim, Y. Y. 2005. "Adapting to a New Culture: An Integrative Communication Theory." In *Theorizing About Intercultural Communication*, edited by W. B. Gudykunst. Sage.

Kluckolm, F., and F. L. Stratbeck. 1961. *Variations in Value Orientations.* Row, Peterson.

Knight, W. M., and K. D. Sweetser. 2021. "Mind the Gap: Understanding Public Relations Competence in the Eyes of Practitioners and the Dominant Coalition." *Public Relations Review* 47 (2).

Kohlburg, L. 1984. *The Psychology of Moral Development.* Harper and Row.

Kolasi, Klevis. 2020. "Structuration Theory." In *The Palgrave Encyclopedia of Global Security Studies*, edited by Scott N. Romaniuk, Péter N. Marton. Palgrave McMillen.

Kozybski, Alfred. 1933. *Science and Sanity: An Introduction to Non-Aristotelian Systems and General Semantics.* The International Non Aristotelian Library Publishing Company.

Kuhn, Thomas, S. (1968). *The Structure of Scientific Revolutions.* University of Chicago Press.

Lane, Anne B. 2020. "The Dialogic ladder: Toward a Framework of Dialogue." *Public Relations Review* 46 (1): 1–8.

Laskin, A. 2012. "Public Relations Scales: Advancing the Excellence Theory." *Journal of Communication Management* 16 (4): 355–370.

Lasswell, H. 1927. *Propaganda Techniques in the World War.* P. Smith.

Lauzen, M. M. 1992. "Public Relations Roles." *Journal of Public Relations Research* 4 (2): 61–80.

Ledingham, John A. 2003. "Explicating Relationship Management as a General Theory of Public Relations." *Public Relations Research* 15 (2): 181–195.

Ledingham, John A. 2006. "Relationship Management: A General Theory of Public Relations." In *Public Relations Theory II*, edited by C. Botan and V. Hazelton. Lawrence Erlbaum Associates.

Lemon, Lauren, L., and Courtney D. Bowman. 2022. "Ethics of Care in Action: Overview of a Holistic Framework with Application to Employee Engagement." *Public Relations Review* 48 (4): 1–9.

Lewin, K. 1943. "Psychology and the Process of Group Living." *Journal of Social Psychology* 17: 113–131.

Lippmann, Walter. 1989. *Public Opinion.* McMillan.

Littlejohn, Stephen W. 1989. *Theories of Human Communication*. 3rd ed. Wadsworth Publishing Company.

Littlejohn, S., and Karen Foss. 2009. "New Media Theory." In *Encyclopedia of Communication Theory*, edited by S. Littlejohn and K. Foss. Sage.

Lowery, S. 1995. *Milestones in Mass Communication Research: Media Effects*. Longman.

Manis, Jerome G., and Bernard N. Melzer. 1978. *Symbolic Interactionism*. Allyn and Bacon.

Marla, R., and C. Callison. 2012. "Absence of Trade Press Coverage of Academic Research: A Bittersweet Victory for Public Relations." *Public Relations Journal* 6 (4).

Marsten, J. 1963. *The Nature of Public Relations*. McGraw Hill.

McCombs, M., and D. Evatt. 1995. "Issues and Attributes: Exploring a New Dimension in Agenda-Setting." *Communicacion y Sociedad* 8: 1–20.

McCombs, M., and D. Shaw. 1972. "The Agenda-Setting Function of the Mass Media." *Public Opinion Quarterly* 36: 176–187.

McCombs, M. E., D. L. Shaw, and D. H. Weaver. 2014. "New Directions in Agenda-Setting Theory and Research." *Mass Communication and Society* 17: 781–802.

McGuire, W. J. 1964. "Inducing Resistance to Persuasion: Some Contemporary Approaches." In *Advances in Experimental Social Psychology*, edited by L. Berkowitz. Academic Press.

McLeod, J. M., and S. Chaffee. 1973. "Interpersonal Approaches to Communication Research." *American Behavioral Scientist* 16 (4): 469–499.

McQuail, D., J. G. Blumler, and J. R. Brown. 1972. "The Television Audience: A Revised Perspective." In *Sociology of Mass Communications*, edited by D. McQuail. Penguin.

McQuail, Denis, and Mark Deuze. 2020. *McQuail's Media and Mass Communication Theory*. 7th ed. Sage.

McWhorter, John. 2021. *Woke Racism: How a New Religion Has Betrayed Black America*. Portfolio.

Meadows, C., and C. W. Meadows III. 2014. "The History of Academic Research in Public Relations: Tracking Research Trends Over Nearly Four Decades." *Public Relations Review* 40: 871–873.

Mehrabian, A., and J. A. Russell. 1974. *An Approach to Environmental Psychology*. MIT Press.

Michaelson, D., and D. W. Stacks. 2011. Standardization in Public Relations Measurement and Evaluation. *Public Relations Journal* 5 (2).

Mikolen, S., B. Quaisen, and J. Wreseke. 2015. "Don't Try Harder: Using Customer Inoculation to Build Resistance Against Service Failures." *Journal of Academy of Marketing Science* 43 (4): 512–527.

Mobaquiao, N. M. 2018. "Speech Act Theory: From Austin to Searle." *Augustinian: A Journal for the Humanities, Social Sciences, Business and Education* 19 (1): 35–45.

Molm, L. D. 1985. "Relative Effects of Individual Dependencies: Further Tests of the Relation Between Power Imbalance and Power Use." *Social Issues* 63 (3): 810–837.

Mundy, Dean E. 2015. "Diversity 2.0: How the Public Relations Function Can Take the Lead in a New Generation of Diversity and Inclusion (D&I) Initiatives." *Research Journal of the Institute for Public Relations* 2 (2).

Mundy, Dean E. 2016. "Bridging the Divide: A Multidisciplinary Analysis of Diversity Research and the Implications for Public Relations." *Research Journal of the Institute for Public Relations* 3 (1).

Myyry, Liisa. 2022. "Moral Judgment and Values." In *Encyclopedia of Violence, Peace and Conflict*. 3rd ed. Vol. 4, edited by Lester R. Kurtz. Elsevier.

Namisango, F., and K. Kang. 2019. "Organization-Public Relationships on Social Media: The Role of Relating Strength, Cohesion and Symmetry." *Computers in Human Behavior* 101: 22–29.

Newcomb, J. M. 1953. "An Approach to the Study of Communicative Acts." *Psychology Review* 60: 393–404.

Noelle-Neumann, E. 1974. "The Spiral of Silence: A Theory of Public Opinion." *Journal of Communication* 24 (2): 43–51.

Noelle-Neumann, Elisabeth. 1984. *The Spiral of Silence: Public Opinion—Our Social Skin*. University of Chicago Press.

O'Keefe, Daniel J. 2016. *Persuasion: Theory and Research*. Sage.

Orlitzky, M., and R. Y. Hirokawa. 2001. "To Err Is Human, to Correct for It Divine: A Meta-Analysis of Research Testing the Functional Theory of Group Decision-Making Effectiveness." *Small Group Research* 32 (3): 313–341.

Page, Tyler G., and Luke W. Capizzo. 2024. "Toward a Tent-Driven Model of Organizations: Stakeholders, Permeability, and Multiple Identities in Public Relations Theory." *Public Relations Review* 50 (1): 1–11.

Palmgreen, Phillip. 1984. "Uses and Gratifications: A Theoretical Perspective." In *Communication Yearbook*, edited by Robert N. Bostrom. Vol. 8. Routledge.

Pang, Augustine, and Yan Jin. 2024. "Theory Advancing Practice: The Contingency Theory in the Strategic Management of Crises, Conflicts and Complex Public Relations Issues." *Public Relations Review* 50 (1).

Parcha, J. M. 2024. "The Theory of Corporate Social Advocacy (CSA) Success: A Guide to CSA Success Using Moral Foundations Theory, Balance Theory, and CSA Authenticity." *International Journal of Business Communication* 1–22.

Pearson, R. 1989. "Business Ethics as Communication Ethics: Public Relations and the Idea of Dialogue." In *Public Relations Theory*, edited by C. Botan and V. Hazleton. Lawrence Erlbaum Associates.

Penning, T. 2008. "First Impressions: U.S. Media Portrayals of Public Relations in the 1920s." *Journal of Communication Management* 12 (4): 344–358.

Penning, T. 2012. "Variance in the RACE Process across PR Practice Settings." *National Communication Association Annual Conference*. Orlando, FL.

Petty, R., and J. T. Cacioppo. 1981. *Attitudes and Persuasion: Classic and Contemporary Approaches*. W.C. Brown and Co.

Petty, R, and J. T. Caciooppo. 1986a. "The Elaboration Likelihood Model of Persuasion." *Advances in Social Psychology* 19: 124–205.

Petty, R., and J. T. Cacioppo. 1986b. *Communication and Persuasion: Central and Peripheral Routes to Attitude Change*. Springer-Verlag.

Pieczka, Magda. 2019. "Looking Back and Going Forward: The Concept of the Public In Public Relations Theory." *Public Relations Inquiry* 1–20.

Poole, Marshall Scott, and Andrea B. Hollingshead. 2005. *Theories of Small Groups: Interdisciplinary Perspectives*. Sage.

Popper, K. R. 1959. *The Logic of Scientific Discovery*. Routledge.

Potter, W. J. 2014. "A Critical Analysis of Cultivation Theory." *Journal of Communication* 64: 1015–1036.

Pressgrove, G., R. McKeever, B. McKeever, and R. C. Waters. 2024. "Investigating Membership Retention: Employing Public Relations Theory to Better Understand Relationship Management." *Journal of Nonprofit and Public Sector Marketing* 36 (1): 1–21.

Prior-Miller, M. 1989. "Four Major Social Scientific Theories and Their Value to the Public Relations Researcher." In *Public Relations Theory*, edited by C. Botan and V. Hazleton. Lawrence Erlbaum Associates.

Prochaska, J. O., S. Johnson, and T. Lee. 1998. "The Trans-Theoretical Model of Behavior Change." In *The Handbook of Health Behavior Change*, edited by E. B. Shumaker, J. K. Schron, and W. L. McBee. Springer Publishing Company.

Public Relations Council. 2024. "Ethics as Culture." *Public Relations Council*. https://prcouncil.net/resources/ethics-as-culture-2/.

Public Relations Society of America. 2021. "Accreditation in Public Relations." *APR Study Guide*. https://www.prsa.org/docs/default-source/accreditation-site/apr-study-guide.pdf?s.

Public Relations Society of America. 2024. "Certificate in Principles of Public Relations." *Public Relations Society of America*. https://accreditation.prsa.org/MyAPR/Content/Apply/Certificate/Certificate.aspx.

Randall, D. 2024. "Implicit Bias Training Hijacks Justice." *Minding the Campus*, December 12. https://www.mindingthecampus.org/2024/12/11/implicit-bias-training-hijacks-justice/#:~:text=Implicit%20bias%20removes%20individual%20intent,of%20individual%20merit%20or%20justice.

Rawlins, B. 2006. "Prioritizing Stakeholders for Public Relations." *Institute for Public Relations*. https://www.instituteforpr.org/wp-content/uploads/2006_Stakeholders_1.pdf.

Rawlins, B. 2008. Measuring the Relationship between Organizational Transparency and Employee Trust. *Public Relations Journal* 2 (2): 1–21.

Rest, J. R. 1986. *Moral Development: Advances in Research and Theory.* Praeger Publishers.

Rogers, C., and V. Andrews. 2013. "Coorientation Theory and Assessment of the RFP Solution to Client Service Learning Matchmaking." *Journalism and Mass Communication Educator* 68 (3): 242–254.

Rogers, E. 1962. *Diffusion of Innovation.* Free Press.

Roy, Debashish. 2020. "Formation of Hofstede's Global Cultural Dimension Index (HGCDI): A Cross-Country Study." *Journal of Transnational Management* 25 (3): 195–224.

Rufo, C. 2023. *America's Cultural Revolution: How the Radical Left Conquered Everything.* Broadside Books.

Schein, Edgar H. 1991. *Organizational Culture and Leadership.* Jossey-Bass Publishers.

Scheufele, D. A. 1999. "Framing as a Theory of Media Effects." *Journal of Communication* 49 (1): 103–122.

Scheufele, D. A., and P. May. 2000. "Twenty-Five Years of Spiral of Silence: A Conceptual Review and Empirical Outlook." *International Journal of Public Opinion Research* 12 (1): 335–354.

Schwartz, Shalom H. 2006. "A Theory of Cultural Value Orientations: Explications and Applications." *Comparative Sociology* 5 (2–3): 137–182.

Sha, B.-L. 2006. "Cultural Identity in the Segmentation of Publics: An Emerging Theory of Intercultural Public Relations." *Journal of Public Relations Research* 18 (1): 45–65.

Sha, Bey-Ling, Qi Wang, and Lan Ni. 2018. *Intercultural Public Relations.* Routledge.

Shannon, Claude, and Warren Weaver. 1949. *Mathematical Theory of Communication.* University of Illinois Press.

Sherif, M., and C. I. Hovland. 1961. *Social Judgment.* Yale University Press.

Shoemaker, Pamela J., and Tim P. Vos. 2009. *Gatekeeping Theory.* Routledge.

Simola, S. 2003. "Ethics of Justice and Care in Corporate Crisis Management." *Journal of Business Ethics* 46 (4): 351–361.

Solomon, D. H., J. R. Dillard, and J. W. Anderson. 2002. "Episode Type, Attachment Orientation, and Frame Salience: Evidence for a Theory of Relational Framing." *Human Communication Research* 28 (1): 136–152.

Staab, P., and T. Thiel. 2022. "Social Media and the Digital Structural Transformation of the Public Sphere." *Theory, Culture, and Society* 39 (4): 129–143.

Stakeholder Theory. n.d. "About". Accessed November 12, 2024. http://stakeholder theory.org/about.

Steele, S. 1998. *The Content of Our Character: A New Vision of Race in America.* Harper Perennial.

Swain, C., and M. Towle. 2023. *The Adversity of Diversity*. Be the People Books.

Tajfel, H. 1981. *Human Groups and Social Categories: Studies in Social Psychology.* Cambridge University Press.

Taylor, Maureen, and Michael Kent. 2014. "Dialogic Engagement: Clarifying Foundational Concepts." *Journal of Public Relations Research* 26 (5): 384–398.

Taylor, M., M. L. Kent, and Y. Xiong. 2019. "Dialog and Organization-Public Relations." In *Public Relations Theory: Application and Understanding*, edited by B. Brunner. Wiley.

Thayer, L. 1968. *Communication and Communication Systems*. Richard D. Irwin.

Thayer, L. 1987. *Communication: Essays in Understanding*. Ablex.

Theunissen, P., and Wan Norbani. 2011. "Revisiting the Concept of 'Dialogue' in Public Relations." *Public Relations Review* 38: 5–13.

Thibaut, J. W., and H. H. Kelley. 1959. *The Social Psychology of Groups.* Transaction Books.

Travis, Eryn, and Edward J. Lordan. 2021. *Public Relations Theory.* Sage.

Tronto, J. C. 1993. *Moral Boundaries: A Political Argument for an Ethics of Care*. Routledge.

van Ruler, Betteke. 2018. "Communication Theory: An Underrated Pillar on Which Strategic Communication Rests." *International Journal of Strategic Communications* 12 (4): 367–381.

Vilagra, Nuvia, Miguel Carbada, and Jose Ruiz San Romain. 2016. "Communicating Corporate Responsibility: Re-Assessment of Classical Theories about Fit between CSR Actions and Corporate Activities." *Communication and Society* 29 (2): 133–146.

Vos, T. P., and F. M. Russell. 2019. "Theorizing Journalism's Institutional Relationships: An Elaboration of Gatekeeping Theory." *Journalism Studies* 20 (16): 2331–2348.

Wakefield, R., and D. Knighton. 2019. "Distinguishing among Publics, Audiences and Stakeholders in the Social Media Era of Unanticipated Publics." *Public Relations Review* 45 (5): 101821.

Walther, J. B. 1992. "Interpersonal Effects in Computer-Mediated Interaction: A Relational Perspective." *Communication Research* 19 (1): 52–90.

Walther, J. B. 1996. "Computer-Mediated Communication: Impersonal, Interpersonal, Hyperpersonal Interaction." *Communication Research* 23 (1): 3–43.

Walther, J. B. 2018. "The Emergence, Convergence, and Resurgence of Intergroup Communication Theory in Computer-Mediated Communication." *Atlantic Journal of Communication* 26 (2): 89–97.

Waters, R. 2009. "Measuring Stewardship in Public Relations: A Test Exploring the Impact on the Fundraising Relationship." *Public Relations Review* 35 (2): 113–119.

Wei, Y., Faye McIntyre, and D. Straub. 2020. "Does Micro Blogging Lead to More Positive Attitude About the Brand? A Perspective of Cultivation Theory." *Journal of Promotion Management* 26 (4): 504–523.

Weiner, B. 1972. "Attribution Theory, Achievement Motivation, and the Educational Process." *Review of Educational Research* 42 (2): 203–215.

Weiner, B. 1995. *Judgments and Responsibility: A Foundation for a Theory of Social Conduct.* Guilford Press.

Western Political Science Association. 2013. "Annual Meeting of Western Political Science Association." http://www.wpsanet.org/papers/docs/Tronto%20WMPSA %20paper%202013.pdf.

White, D. M. 1950. "The 'Gate Keeper': A Case Study in the Selection of News." *Journalism Quarterly* 27 (4): 383–391.

Wills, Caitlin M. 2020. "Diversity in Public Relations: The Implications of a Broad Definition for PR Practice." *Public Relations Journal* 13 (3).

Windahl, S., B. Signitzer, and J. Olson. 2007. *Using Communication Theory.* 2nd ed. Sage.

Wirtz, J. G., and T. M. Zimbras. 2018. "A Systemic Analysis of Research Applying 'Principles of Dialogic Communication' to Organizational Websites, Blogs, and Social Media: Implications for Theory and Practice." *Journal of Public Relations Research* 30 (1–2): 5–34.

Witmer, D. F. 2006. "Overcoming System Boundaries." In *Public Relations Theory II*, edited by C. Botan and V. Hazleton. Lawrence Erlbaum Associates.

Woodson, R., ed. 2021. *Red, White and Black: Rescuing American History from Revisionists and Race Hustlers.* Emancipation Books.

Xu, Mengyao, Fritz Cropp, and Glen T. Cameron. 2023. "Dissecting Moral Judgments: Using Moral Foundation Theory to Advance the Contingency Continuum." *Public Relations Review* 49 (4): 102370.

Yook, B. and D. W. Stacks. 2024. "Should CEO Be the 'Face' of Crisis Response? Examining Type of Visuals on Social Media in Corporate Crisis Communication." *Journal of Contingencies in Crisis Management* 32 (3): e12596.

About the Author

Dr. Timothy Penning, PhD, APR, Fellow PRSA, is a tenured full professor in the School of Communication at Grand Valley State University in Allendale, Michigan. A former journalist and public relations professional, he now teaches undergraduate and graduate courses in public relations writing, management, ethics and law, and communication management. Dr. Penning is the author of several public relations textbooks as well as book chapters and numerous journal articles. His research is related to the theme of influences on public relations content, and topics include corporate communication team performance, investor relations, nonprofit annual reports, public relations capacity on organizational boards, and value perceptions of public relations career achievements. He does some public relations consulting and blogs about issues in the public relations profession.

Index

www.ingramcontent.com/pod-product-compliance
Lightning Source LLC
Chambersburg PA
CBHW061307220326
41599CB00026B/4773